BUILDING A LEARNING ORGANIZATION:

BUILDING A LEARNING ORGANIZATION:

▼

7 Lessons to Involve Your CEO

Edited by Jeanne C. Meister

iUniverse.com, Inc.

San Jose New York Lincoln Shanghai

Building a Learning Organization:
7 Lessons to Involve Your CEO

All Rights Reserved © 2001 by Jeanne C. Meister

Published by iUniverse.com, Inc.

For information address:
iUniverse.com, Inc.
5220 S 16th, Ste. 200
Lincoln, NE 68512
www.iuniverse.com

ISBN: 0-595-18484-7

Printed in the United States of America

CONTENTS

PREFACE

This book evolved from an original work known as "Learning From The CEO: How Chief Executive Officers Shape Corporate Education." In that book, seven companies were interviewed by their respective Chief Learning Officer and profiled in individual case studies. These seven companies devoted tremendous time, resources and effort to capture the best practices of how to involve a CEO in the learning process. These original seven companies include:

Bain & Company
Buckman Laboratories
Dell Computer Corporation
Deutsche Bank
STMicroelectroincs
Tennessee Valley Authority
United Technologies

But when the original book was published it was written as a series of case studies instead of concrete lessons everyone training manager could follow in order to involve the CEO in the learning process. Hence I made the decision to re-write the book and make it more user-friendly, detailing the lessons in leaning to get top management involvement.

The book also includes a special section on the Corporate University Xchange website (found at www.corpu.com) include dedicated background material on the subject of management support and involvement for learning, a Power Point presentation of best practices of CEO involvement in learning, as well as a list of companies which have been identified as having Learning CEOs.

The new and improved book could not have been possible without the many people who worked with me to create the final manuscript. First I am indebted to Dana Isaacson, Executive Editor at Corporate University Xchange who served as project manager and coach. Tom Fitch entered the project and was instrumental in providing new content, as well as shaping the final product: turning a massive collection of words into a well written easy to read book. Finally, Matt Panetta, Research Associate, played a key role in researching and identifying the Learning CEOs that were ultimately included in the book.

Additionally, I would like to acknowledge the original seven CEOs and their Chief Learning Officers and their staff who got this book off to a start and shared their time and expertise in identifying how to involve the CEO.

Bain & Company	Tom Tierney, Managing Director, Steven Tallman
Buckman Laboratories,	Bob Buckman, CEO, Michelle Means, Sheldon Ellis and Alison Tucker
Dell Computer	Michael Dell, CEO and John Coné, President Dell Learning
Deutsche Bank	Rolf Breuer, CEO and Martin Moehrle and Michael Maffucci;
STMicroelectronics	Pasquale Pistorio, CEO and Jean-Claude Nataf, and Jean-Philippe Dauvin

Tennessee Valley Authority	Craven Crowell, former CEO and John Turner, Mary Catherine Hammon, Lynn Hodges and James Thornton
United Technologies	George David, CEO and Woody Exley and Larry Gavrich

Thank you again for inspiring me to bring this project to fruition.

On a final note, I would like to thank Tina Sung, President of American Society for Training & Development, Nancy Olson, Director of Education, and Ruth Stadius, Manager of Book Publishing, for the approval to co-publish this book with ASTD Press. This ensures that the greatest number of practitioners will have an opportunity to read the book and join our network.

—Jeanne Meister, March 2001

CHAPTER ONE:

▼

THE CEO AS
CORPORATE EDUCATOR

"The hiring and employee development process has deep ramifications for the future of an organization. Many executives have neglected a personal involvement, accountability and initiative in developing leaders. Because this process is full of unknowns, it deserves more time than anything else a CEO does."

—Larry Bossidy, former Chairman, CEO, Allied Signal

Every day, chief executive officers and their boards of directors around the globe are faced with tough investment decisions. They sign off on mega-mergers, as America Online did with Time Warner, or they launch new business models, as Michael Dell did in 1984 with his then revolutionary direct-to-customer model. As investors, these CEOs base their decisions on tangible results geared to increasing shareholder value.

In the 1980s and 1990s, CEOs focused their attention on understanding information technology investments, which ran the gamut from Y2K compliance to developing Internet capabilities and building e-businesses. Unquestionably, these investments required CEOs to get their arms around information technology issues that often presented significant obstacles. These obstacles ranged from the difficulty of estimating costs that often changed in midstream to defining benefits that may or may not materialize. Over the last 20 years, CEOs have increasingly made information technology a key part of their agenda. In fact, CEOs are routinely managing their information technology strategy as an investment that will build new capabilities rather than a cost to improve current operations. In other words, information technology has become a critical element of not just keeping the organization competitive but also positioning it properly for the future.

Enter the CEO agenda for the 21st century. While information technology has been elevated to the ranks of a top-priority for the organization, understanding the organization's commitment and investment in education has now joined IT as a high priority for the organization. In fact, a growing number of CEOs are becoming increasingly committed to developing new and innovative learning programs and sharing these with the investment community. For example, when George David, CEO of United Technologies Corporation (UTC), announced the revolutionary Employee Scholar Program to security analysts in 1995, he said, "We want to have the best educated work force on the planet." The Employee Scholar Program was designed to prepay tuition and fees for all employees, give employees paid time off for study, and upon graduation present each employee an award of company stock worth $10,000.

This level of commitment by United Technologies is unique. But it's totally consistent with the philosophy of George David, the enlightened CEO who said in 1995, "We have the Employee Scholar Program because I believe education is the single biggest discriminating factor between fear of job loss and anticipation of job change. We want our employees to be on the offensive. We want our employees to think about their own lives, to control their own lives and to realize there cannot ever be employment guarantees. Employment guarantees are bad for society. We want people to embrace the future and they do that with education."

Today, more than 12,000 UTC hourly and salaried employees are graduates of the Employee Scholar Program, more than double the number of just four years ago. Traditionally, there has been a fear that allowing employees to acquire new knowledge and skills might encourage them to find new jobs. But the experience at United Technologies has demonstrated the opposite. In fact, in recent years the turnover rate for employees who graduated from the Employee Scholar Program has been only half the rate for the work force as a whole. The commitment from David is typical of how an involved CEO leads a commitment to learning so that the rest of the management team and the corporation as a whole will understand the urgency of making education part of the CEO agenda.

The vision of George David is just one example of what this book profiles; *Building A Learning Organization* details how education has become a top priority at many organizations and focuses primarily on Dell Computer Corporation, Bain & Company, Buckman Laboratories, Deutsche Bank, STMicroelectronics, Tennessee Valley Authority, and United Technologies Corporation. However, this book does more than present lessons learned. What emerges is a blueprint for how and why CEOs are investing in corporate education. The many CEOs profiled here manage education for value creation, and, importantly they ask the same questions about investing in education that they do with any investment, such as:

- What is our total investment in our people?
- How will this investment increase shareholder value?
- How does an investment in our people compare with our competitors' investment in their people?

At the same time the CEOs question their investment in education, the dollar amount of this investment has grown substantially. In fact, the average investment at the seven firms mentioned above is $20 million per year. Quite simply, for most organizations there is little room for debate—their investment in people must be treated as any other investment, put on the CEO agenda, and managed not as a cost but as an investment which will build new capabilities and create competitive advantage for the organization.

What Can Your CEO Do?

The most well known example of CEO involvement in continuous learning is General Electric's Jack Welch—the poster boy for commitment and investment in learning. Welch's mantra is simply that, "An organization's ability to learn and translate that learning into action rapidly is the ultimate competitive advantage." Welch has made an enormous commitment to becoming involved as a teacher at Crotonville, the corporate university of General Electric. Welch visits Crotonville twice each month, lecturing to GE executives and mingling at receptions for more informal one-to-one conversations. In total, Welch speaks to roughly 1,000 executives a year through his teaching at Crotonville—an impressive commitment to learning for a Fortune 100 CEO.

Within the last three and one half years, Welch's commitment to learning has also included his involvement in adopting Six Sigma across General Electric. Six Sigma is the statistical measure that expresses how close a product comes to its quality goal. General Electric built its quality program on the Motorola model, the first company to use Six Sigma in the late 1980s.

Since adopting the Six Sigma model in 1996, Welch describes Six Sigma as "moving the organization from a commitment to a training program to becoming fundamentally responsible for changing the DNA of the entire company." The numbers are quite impressive indeed. In the last three and a half years, while General Electric invested $500 million in training its workforce in Six Sigma—with three weeks of training and one Six Sigma project under the belt of every employee—it has produced amazing financial returns. The savings in 1998 from Six Sigma projects totaled more than $750 million over and above GE's investment. The savings is expected to rise above $1 billion and Welch has predicted billions more would be saved in increased volume and market share.

Of course most people don't work for General Electric, their CEO is not Jack Welch. What can they do to get their CEO involved in learning? While a growing number of annual reports boast, "Our people are our most important asset," how many CEOs are directly involved as teachers, as Jack Welch has been at General Electric? How many are on the interview team to recruit and hire a new chief learning officer?

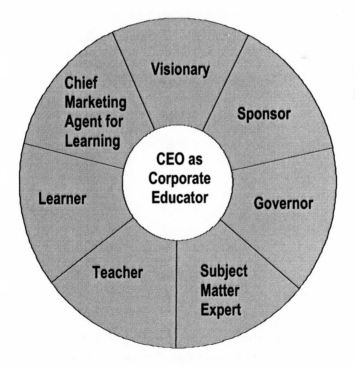

Figure 1-1: The CEO as Corporate Educator 2001, Corporate University Xchange

While a committed CEO who rolls up his/her sleeves and gets actively involved in teaching is invaluable to developing a "learning organization," the fact remains that few CEOs do this. So what do the committed CEOs profiled in this book actually do and why have they become so involved in learning? A model developed by Corporate University Xchange (Figure 1-1) identifies seven key characteristics exemplified by the CEO as corporate educator:

1. *CEO as Visionary.* Presents a clear direction for corporate learning around which the organization can rally.

2. *CEO as Sponsor.* Provides encouragement, resources, and commitment for strategic learning to flourish and develop; sponsors groundbreaking new learning programs.

3. *CEO as Governor.* Takes an active role in governing the corporate learning function, reviews goals and objectives, provides direction on how to measure the effectiveness of learning, and evaluates outcomes.

4. *CEO as Subject Matter Expert.* Actively takes on the role of thought leader and develops new learning programs for the entire organization.

5. *CEO as Teacher.* Teaches programs on-site and/or provides resources to create online learning platforms that are used to deliver new enterprise-wide learning programs.

6. *CEO as Learner.* Becomes the role model for lifelong learning for the entire organization and acknowledges his/her willingness to constantly learn.

7. *CEO as Chief Marketing Agent.* Promotes the company's commitment to learning by mentioning it in speeches, the annual report, press interviews, reports to security analysts and general marketing

tools such as posters, e-mail messages and articles in the company magazine.

The examples below identify specific ways CEOs are involved in learning. These best practices are meant to provide a roadmap of exactly what a CEO does to further the learning culture. It is also designed to shorten the discovery process for enlightened deans of corporate universities and training directors who want to involve their CEO in shaping a learning culture.

The CEO as Visionary

Thomas Tierney, Bain & Company's former worldwide managing director, is the leading advocate for shaping and articulating Bain's learning vision, which is to "Create the best environment in the world for learning how add value to businesses." Tierney's passion for learning is reflected in his vision of Bain as a global community of "teacher-learners." Tierney believes these teacher-learners share several characteristics, such as:

- Being actively engaged in teaching, probing and learning—all simultaneously.
- Demonstrating care for their colleagues, and making intellectual and emotional connections in and beyond their circle of peers.
- Relating to as many people from different backgrounds, experience, and maturity levels/positions as possible. This is what Tierney calls "nurturing the bandwidth capacity."
- Reflecting on what they have learned as well as how they learn. After learning or teaching, these teacher-learners ask themselves, "What have I learned about learning? What should I explore to enrich my own learning as a result of this interaction?"
- Keeping their receiver-transmitters on at all times. Teacher-learners possess a child's mind; they don't presuppose, they listen.

As Tierney sees it, teacher-learners are made not born. A teacher-learner profile is the product of role models, parents, friends, and experiences and of course, the organization itself, which nurtures and rewards such characteristics. Tierney's legacy will be to create a professional service organization where each employee can become both a teacher and a learner.

Defining this vision for learning has also spilled over into Bain's consulting practice. Tierney has pressed the firm to ask such questions as: How do you design your plant, your facilities and even your floor plan for learning? How do you set up and manage client interactions for learning? How do you go about recruiting and hiring people who are both teachers and learners? How do you sustain a teacher-learner approach in the context of instant obsolescence of learning?

By identifying a strong vision for learning, Tierney provides the Bain community of 2,000 employees and 1,500 clients with a clear mandate for how learning is a strategic necessity for the firm.

The CEO as Sponsor

Dr. Rolf Breuer, CEO for Deutsche Bank has been a vocal sponsor for crafting a new executive education practice within Deutsche Bank. In fact Dr. Breuer recognized that a new learning paradigm for executive education was needed if Deutsche Bank was to achieve its strategic business goals. What Dr. Breuer eventually created is known as the Spokesman's Challenge, a partnership between Deutsche Bank and Duke University. Twenty participants form various business divisions were invited to the kick-off an executive education program that starts with Dr. Breuer asking the group four key questions which revolved around matrix management, knowledge management, globalization and innovation. The questions posed to the group included:

- What are the cultural and organizational characteristics of a global firm?

- What are the characteristics of successful matrix organizations? What should the Bank do in order to get maximum benefit from its matrix organization?

- What needs to change for Deutsche Bank to become more innovative and entrepreneurial? How do these changes occur?

- How can Deutsche Bank better mange knowledge as a critical resource for business success?

Once the four challenges were framed, the participants were divided into four mixed teams. Each team tackled one of the four challenges. The entire Spokesman's Challenge group met with the sponsor, Rolf Breuer, at roughly six-week intervals. The personal involvement of Deutsche Bank's CEO had a lasting impact on Challenge program participants. "The time we spent with Dr. Breuer was quality time" says one manager. "It gave us a real opportunity to understand, at a level none of us was previously familiar with, the scope of strategic issues that the Executive Board has to deal with. The time spent with Dr. Breuer also made clear to us that the issues we were addressing were integral to the continued success of the firm. We really did feel that we were part of the process."

A few weeks after the program began, Deutsche Bank publicly announced the acquisition of Bankers Trust. Most of the Spokesman's Challenge participants became deeply involved in the integration planning within their respective business lines. Many of these managers asked themselves if they could personally continue to participate in the program in light of the additional pressure the Bankers Trust integration was placing on their daily workload.

The executive management group that took on this challenge used this an opportunity to bring new perspectives as well as a new vision statement to the Bankers Trust/Deutsche Bank merger. Dr. Breuer became the most prominent and visible sponsor of executive education within the Bank. Now customized executive programs like the Duke University partnership are the norm for Deutsche Bank. They are seen as critical to not only developing the leadership and management competencies of the business leaders but also producing tangible results.

While Dr. Breuer's name is equated with The Spokesman Challenge, the same degree of sponsorship inspired Dr. Bob Buckman to develop a knowledge management system in the mid 1980s well before it became a buzz word in the business world. These were also the days when e-mail was rudimentary, the Internet was largely unknown, and there was no World Wide Web. Dr. Buckman became a believer in knowledge sharing—a belief that the gathering of all the tacit knowledge of all Buckman associates is the most powerful weapon for progress, innovation, and competitive advantage. Buckman Laboratories committed itself to its customers, associates and business allies by creating K'Netix, the Buckman Knowledge Network.

Since over 86 percent of Buckman associates work outside the office in most of the 90-plus countries in which the company does business, Buckman realized it was imperative that he develop a system to connect these associates so that their knowledge was accessible to one another. K'Netix allows all Buckman associates to participate in virtual discussion groups around the flow of industry specific and general company information. At the heart of K'Netix is the Knowledge Nurture web site where subject matter experts at Buckman Laboratories get in touch with one another and help solve customer problems, design new programs, or give advice on engineering better systems. (You can see this for yourself at www.knowledge-nurture.com.) Buckman believed from the earliest stages that by creating this knowledge management system he was differentiating Buckman Labs from the competition.

The CEO as Governor

Michael Dell showed his involvement in learning when he insisted on being included in the interview team when it came time to hire a new head of Dell Learning. Recalling the interview, John Coné, Dell's head of learning says, "I have to admit that the first time I met Michael, I was impressed with how engaged he was on the topic of corporate education. He spent as much time asking me what he could do as he did asking what I expected to bring to the function."

Michael Dell believes that management, especially senior management, must be the champions of education for the company and manage education strategically. Because of this commitment to become involved in the strategic issues related to Dell Learning, Michael Dell created the Dell Learning Board of Regents, whose mission is to set policy, support, direct, and review the operation of education within the Dell Corporation. The members of this board include the vice presidents of three major operating groups, along with the vice presidents of finance and human resources and the president of Dell Learning, who serves as a non-voting member and secretary to the board. The meetings are intended to accomplish the following ten results:

- Review and approve company-wide budget and conformity to budget
- Establish standards, budgets, and strategic direction for Dell Learning
- Review and approve resources for annual regional education plans
- Review measurement of training effectiveness
- Review utilization of facilities
- Review information technology requirements for learning
- Review new education priorities and build vs. buy proposals
- Review course maintenance proposals
- Understand delivery strategies and set goals for coming year
- Hear presentations by Dell Learning staff on new initiatives

At Dell, the following decisions were made by the CEO and Board of Regents in the first year of Dell Learning's existence:

All Dell employees will have a training plan that spells out learning required for their job; All managers are required to have education plans for their organizations that reflect the competencies required in their business.

Dell Learning will move to tuition-based education in order to put control of key decision about learning in the hands of the end users

Dell Learning will set a goal for 40 percent non-classroom training (the goal for 1999 was 70 percent and moving upward).

While Michael Dell was the driving force behind launching the Board of Regents and served as one of its governors, as time has passed decisions concerning training have become a natural part of management activities. Today, items once handled by the board are part of the regular executive committee agenda. Michael Dell's contribution has been significant—education is now an important part of the CEO agenda.

The CEO as Subject Matter Expert

While every CEO is qualified as an expert in many aspects of the company's business, Michael Dell is unique as both the founder of the company and the inventor of the direct-to-customer business model. As such, Michael has become the chief subject matter expert and he has developed an online training program known as The Dell Business Model. At the heart of the direct-to-customer model is eliminating the middleman and other unnecessary costs involved in selling computers to end users.

The Dell business model online training course was developed through extensive interviews with Michael Dell recounting the evolution of the model and clarifying its basic tenets. Based upon these interviews, a draft of the course content was written. Michael Dell carefully reviewed each word and sometimes re-wrote entire sections. The resulting program, known as "Michael Dell Says" allows learners to hear about key aspects of the Dell business model in the founder's own words. There are also "dig downs" that allow each learner to learn more by accessing supplemental materials. Today, countless presentations and training tools have been derived from that single program authored by Michael Dell.

The CEO as Teacher

Perhaps the most important theme linking these CEOs is their active involvement as teacher and strategic guiding force for corporate education. In many cases, this means the CEO gets involved directly as an instructor or facilitator in formal educational courses. Take the example of George David, CEO of United Technologies. David co-facilitates a course in leadership at the Darden School of Business at the University of Virginia, the educational partner for UTC in executive education and development. (In 1999 Business week ranked Darden No. 1 among business schools worldwide in providing customized programs to corporations.) Several times a year David travels to Charlottesville, Virginia, to meet and exchange ideas with UTC managers enrolled in the Emerging Leaders course.

This program is based on UTC's business priorities and taught by Darden faculty. Each UTC manager comes to the program with a personal leadership project that is developed over the course of three weeks. This project ranges from developing a new pricing model to improving cycle time or creating a new communications plan. David also encourages other senior UTC leaders, such as Karl Krapek, president and COO and Steven Page, president of Otis Elevator Company, to facilitate this program. David believes that the success of the Emerging Leadership program depends upon direct links to the top leadership of the company.

Not every CEO is an active classroom teacher like George David. Some, like Craven Crowell of TVA, teach by example and become the de facto chief learning officer, supporting education and motivating senior line managers to become involved in education. This is where TVA University comes in. Dr. John Turner, senior vice president for education, training and diversity, built the groundwork and conferred with Crowell about how a CEO can become involved in learning and specifically what it means for a CEO to operate as a chief learning officer. This was then followed by having TVA University develop a course entitled Developing Leaders, an experiential "train-the-trainer" program intended to set guideline for how TVA managers can serve as faculty for TVA University. This program certifies TVA managers as faculty and regularly evaluates them on their performance as faculty, providing specific feedback on how to improve as teachers and mentors.

TVA managers serving as faculty operate either in a classroom or as subject mater experts on video. TVA's chief financial officer, David Smith, recently appeared in an instructional video for the TVA University course, *TVA Finances: Dollars and Decisions*. In this video, Smith explains TVA's finances and how the organization makes money; the video simplifies the company's complex financial picture. The result for TVA is a more relevant learning experience.

The concept of training managers to be faculty has also taken hold in Europe, as exemplified by STMicroelectronics' ST University (STU). STU has developed a formal program known as ST Trains ST; by the end of 1999 this certification program trained more than 200 STMicroelectronics' managers to be STU faculty. Once these managers are certified as ST faculty, they become involved as facilitators of training programs, teaching workshops for roughly five to 10 percent of their total work time. STMicroelectronics has more than 100 locations in 24 countries, and this decentralized learning model allows the company to set up local centers of excellence around the globe.

The CEO as Learner

Perhaps the most impressive example of the CEO as learner can be seen in the impact Thomas Tierney, Bain & Company's former worldwide managing director, has had by insisting that the Bain training organization use the same "outside-inside" approach to learning that is at the core of its consulting practice. For Tierney, "outside-in" learning means this "out-side-in learning," meaning bringing the academy into Bain. Tierney makes this happen by creating a Bain Academy where the "best of Bain" thinkers and consultants search for and digest relevant business insights and apply these to Bain consulting assignments and to Bain Training and Development activities.

But Tierney puts his beliefs into action by enlisting a cadre of Bain consultants as the teachers and faculty for the outside-in approach to learning. Tierney is adamant about committing Bain's case team and firm leadership to facilitating programs. As Tierney says, "Our consultant trainer pool will grow in proportion to the numbers we have to train. It is and will continue to be expensive. But consider the value. Our internal data shows that our partners rank being a trainer as one of the most outstanding activities of their careers. I believe consultants, managers and senior partners should provide the bulk of the trainer pool since this is the way to integrate them into the firm's goals and values."

The CEO as Chief Marketing Agent for Learning

The CEOs profiled here believe their role is to personally embody their organization's learning principles. Tierney of Bain sees himself as the "public face" of Bain and its Bain Virtual University. To Tierney, this means, "being a frequent contributor to business journals commenting not only on business strategy, the heart of the Bain consulting practice but also on trends in learning and knowledge management. Internally it is not uncommon for Tierney to send firm-wide e-mails announcing a new Bain Virtual University program or other key learning initiative. He also believes it is his role to clone other Bain leaders to take an active role in learning and supporting learning among their direct reports. .

This public commitment to learning is also displayed by Andy Grove, Intel's chief executive. Grove wrote an entire book devoted to the subject entitled, *High Output Management*. In the book he shares his philosophy of commitment to employee education in the chapter entitled, "Why Training is the Boss's Job." Here, Grove describes the importance of his involvement in employee education and development as a prerequisite for the company's survival. While Intel has a relatively young workforce, most of the technologies used in Intel's blockbuster Pentium chip did not exist when the scientists and engineers finished their graduate studies. Without recruiting the best brains in the business and without continually making large investments in their education and training, Intel would not have been able to stay on the cutting edge of technology.

Beyond writing books on the importance of education and training, CEOs are also sharing their commitment to educating their workforce in the company annual report and in speeches to security analysts. A Corporate University Xchange research report, *Survey of Corporate University Future Directions* (involving 120 deans of top corporate education organizations) found that 57 percent of the publicly traded companies report the contribution of their education and training strategy in the company annual report. For example, Conoco, the international energy company, recently returned to the New York Stock Exchange after 17 years as a subsidiary of DuPont and in its first annual report, the company devoted several paragraphs to the contributions Conoco University has made to developing visionary leaders.

Learning From CEOs:
The Benefits to Your Organization

The reputation of these best practice corporate universities has increasingly become a key source of the company's competitive advantage in recruiting and retaining the best graduates. The company case studies that follow point to lowered employee turnover rates and notable examples of how employees have risen from administrative assistant positions to middle management positions, and in the process have developed their self-confidence at both work and in their personal lives. For example, in the last five years Bain & Company has experienced increased rates of employee retention and higher levels of employee satisfaction, attributed in great part to the extensive learning opportunities at the firm.

Another key benefit profiled by our best practice organizations is the global integration of learning as "one organization." Deutsche Bank, Dell Computer, and Buckman Laboratories all operating across the world have stressed the importance of learning as one firm. This means that embedded within all the training programs are shared values and a shared culture in which employees around the world can participate and, in some cases, actually become certified in.

As a group, these CEOs are taking a leap of faith and becoming involved in the education and development of their employees. The CEO as chief corporate educator extends beyond thinking about and promoting the learning function. These CEOs figure prominently as learning visionaries and teachers, sharing their insights about the company, the industry, the competitors, and the strategic direction of the organization. What these CEOs are really doing is building the intellectual capital of their respective organizations through their involvement in corporate-wide learning.

Lesson #1

Create and promote a vision for learning.

Chapter Two:

—————▼—————

The CEO as Visionary

"True learning must be re-imaged to extend through and beyond traditional training strategies to encompass radically new learning models."
—*Tom Tierney, Former Worldwide Managing Director Bain & Company*

The CEO is the public face of the organization, the person most identified with the corporation by employees, investors and the public at large. The CEO is often referred to as the chief spokesman, chief strategist and visionary. But in numerous organizations profiled in this book, the CEO is emerging as the chief advocate for learning. When the CEO becomes the "Chief Education Officer," he or she is an advocate for shaping and articulating the organization's learning vision, and integrating that learning vision with the organization's business direction.

As companies recognize the value of a well-trained workforce, CEO support for learning and corporate training is gathering steam. Some CEOs are vocal advocates of learning and have helped to give shape and definition to their corporate learning initiatives. These executives support their organizations' learning activities by taking an active role in drafting their company's learning mission and by meeting frequently with managers to help bring that vision into reality. Thomas Tierney, former CEO of Bain & Co., a management consulting firm, states the CEO's role in education and learning is simply to "create the best environment in the world for learning how to add value to business."

Corporate learning is inevitably tied to company mission. Jack Welch, the chief executive of General Electric who guided GE's transformation from manufacturer to diversified multinational corporation in less than 15 years, achieved that remarkable accomplishment by focusing GE's resources on businesses where GE was the number one or number two competitor. Recognizing the value of the individual employee, Welch initiated a program he called "Work-Out" to move decision-making closer to GE business units and get GE employees involved. "Work-Out has made us faster and more open to ideas from anywhere, and, as a result, cracked the back of bureaucracy, got everyone involved, and made us a much better company," Welch said in a 1999 company memo.

Another Welch initiative, soon after taking over as CEO in 1981, was to elevate the importance of GE's corporate education center, Crotonville, as a training ground for GE's rising star managers. Thousands of GE managers, after taking part in Crotonville's Core Leadership Development Program, have brought back to their business units the company's core values—passion for excellence, openness to ideas, confidence in themselves and their fellow employees, to name a few—and became messengers for transferring these values to other GE workers. [1]

What is the role of the CEO as Visionary for learning?

CEOs who are visionaries for learning are actively shaping the learning development and strategy in their organizations. This doesn't necessarily mean these CEOs play a hands-on role in course design and courseware management, but that they are involved in articulating the learning vision for the organization. For example, the CEO creates an environment where learning and knowledge sharing can take root across the organization. Some, including General Electric's Jack Welch, are both learning visionaries and hands-on instructors.

The universe of CEOs who take an active role in guiding enterprise-wide learning, or who are beginning to assume that role, appears to be growing, according to interviews with chief learning officers at a wide range or organizations. Even so, activist CEOs who play a visible role in corporate learning are still in the minority. Only about 20% of corporate CEOs say they perform an active role in setting company strategy, according to a survey of 160 CEOs.[2] The majority of CEOs prefer having strategy decisions made by people closer to the business units, the managers who actually run these businesses.

Chief executives of the following companies: Bain & Company, Buckman Laboratories, Dell Computer, General Electric, and Memorial Herman Healthcare System, are among the growing number of CEOs taking active roles in setting the learning vision in their organizations. Several talk openly about their efforts in building a "learning organization," an environment in which employees will want to share ideas and learn from each other.

Bain's Learning Vision:
Learning Locally and Teaching Globally

Bain & Company, one of the largest top-tier strategy consulting firms, maintains 26 offices around the world and employs over 2,400 consultants and administrative staff. Since its founding in 1973 Bain has worked with more than 1,500 clients, engaging in work ranging from development and implementation of corporate business strategy to customer retention, cost reduction, portfolio assessment and process re-engineering.

Early on, Bain established a reputation for creating results for clients, not just reports. "This was the original partners' defining vision," says

Thomas Tierney, Bain's worldwide managing director (the equivalent title for CEO). "It meant then, and it still holds true, that we work with our clients in developing practical strategies that succeed in the marketplace." Bain parts company with many other consulting firms in that it rotates consultants through a variety of assignments, bucking the industry's trend toward specialization. Bain consultants are encouraged to develop a broadly defined set of management consulting skills.

Under Tierney's guidance, Bain has discovered its learning vision: "To create the best environment in the world where talented people learn how to add value to businesses." This learning vision is put into action through a network of teacher-learners, enabling Bain consultants to learn from each other, sharing best practices in a real-time fashion from anywhere in the world. Bain effectively became a training ground for people who think and act like general managers, entrepreneurs, and innovators.

"We're convinced that these three roles form the bedrock of competitive advantage," affirms Steven Tallman, Bain's former vice president of training. "Consequently, our learning strategy involves skill mastery and modeling. It means integrating the knowledge, skills, and personal behaviors Bain consultants need to master and model to help their clients outperform their competitors. Our job—whether it's through formal training, or coaching, or experience-sharing—is to help them let the heart and soul of the general manager get into their DNA," adds Tallman.

Bain's commitment to client competitive advantage drives the company's learning approach to guarantee that Bain people learn and apply the knowledge and skills necessary to succeed in (1) advising businesses on strategy and implementation; (2) managing businesses; and (3) investing in businesses and innovative products and services.

Tierney probably has made the greatest impact on learning at Bain in his role as visionary. Interpreting ongoing business trends, particularly those affecting professional service firms, he views corporate learning in the context of businesses moving away from the product-driven enterprise to the talent and knowledge-driven enterprise. "In professional services and knowledge-based businesses—take software, for example—value is created by talented people creating and applying knowledge," he suggests. This movement is detected in a paradigm shift away from machines to people, and from products to knowledge. As Tierney sees it, the challenge for any professional service firm, and for Bain in particular, is to attract and retain the right kind of people and to work with them to create "real-time" applied knowledge.

At Bain, Tierney has become dedicated to forming what he calls "Constellation Leadership." His use of an astronomical metaphor is quite apt. "In building 'Constellation Leadership' in professional services," he says, "you have to create stars. It is a recruiting essential, a development opportunity, and a retention challenge. We're constantly going after the stars, the top quartile of the talent pool. Our principal leadership task at Bain is to take that individual star, create networks to get the star talking with other stars, and provide incentives to encourage that star to stay with us. If we get all that right, we then can encourage the stars to accelerate learning throughout the system. But that's where true value is created nowadays. It's a totally different way of making money than the industry models many companies have been using for decades."[3]

To achieve "Constellation Leadership," Tierney has worked with the Bain management team to determine eight fundamental principles for managing knowledge and learning at the firm. They are known as "Tierney's Eight Learning Principles," and can be described as:

1. *The only good learning is practical learning.* Practical learning generates results. It creates commercial value for customers and clients. "In our business," Tierney states, "only applied knowledge is relevant. And we define 'applied knowledge' as 'only what is practical to help a client achieve his strategic goals.'"

2. *The shelf life of knowledge is declining rapidly.* The case-specific applications of what consultants learn are riddled with the inevitability of obsolescence. Consequently, most learning must be done in real

time. The learning environment must be organized for just-in-time learning that targets just-in-time applications.

3. *Learning occurs in diverse communities of interaction, especially across many cultures.* Tierney anchors his passion for learning in his experience as a leadership and strategy consultant. "You can't begin to think of yourself as an insightful strategist, let alone a cutting-edge leader, if you don't see your enterprise as a community of 'teacher-learners.'"

4. *Communities of learning require significant and intentional investment.* The company has to invest intentionally in promoting and supporting learning among "stars" in communities of interaction, especially as these stars relate to each other and talk to each other in endlessly permuting groupings. Tierney maintains that "communities of interaction" are constantly forming and re-forming at points of contact. These contact points may be either managed or occur *ad hoc.* "You have to look at these communities of interaction as organisms," Tierney suggests. "When it comes to interacting, they are porous. They are constantly changing, morphing, and subdividing. In other words, they are a perpetual series of virtual conversations among diverse 'experts' using diverse media in diverse settings."

5. *The nature of Bain's business demands personalized learning, a burden shared by both the organization and the individual.* At Bain, *personalized* learning is valued over *codified* learning. "Looking at how management consultants use technology," Tierney says, "you can think of a computer database as a storehouse of information and accumulated corporate experience. The consultant uses his computer to access this database warehouse. This is codified learning. And it is a weakness of current approaches to Knowledge Management. These approaches focus on systems, and not on interactions between people, where learning really takes place." Tierney contrasts codified learning with personalized learning. "We prefer personalized learning. This means

that our consultants use computers and other electronic media to *communicate* knowledge, not *store* it. We think computers exist to create 'learning moments,' to facilitate dialogue and conversation, to get us talking and to add value to our interaction."

6. *Learning in a talent-driven enterprise is highly strategic.* Professional service organizations like Bain rely on the rigor with which they capture and apply knowledge. As Tierney explains, "We have to have the right people who are learning the right things in the right client relationships and at the optimal cost for the value generated. And I say 'optimal' and not 'lowest' cost because we're willing to invest where we see the value."

7. *The only valuable technology is technology that enables practical learning.* Tierney is aware of the tension that exists between technology as a facilitator of learning and technology as an an enabler of information overload. Technology that facilitates learning makes access to the right knowledge easier.

Considering the accelerating obsolescence of learning, he suggests that professional service firms like Bain & Company make questioning the status quo just the way they do business. Tierney, however, tempers his appetite for change with a cautionary note: "By all means, drive the organization to create. But our business pushes us to be more adaptive than inventive. There is little institutional value to the first mover. Consequently, we build our business around sifting, synthesizing, and adapting. We are adaptive learning leaders."

Tierney's guiding vision led to several company-wide education and training initiatives: the Bain Worldwide Training Advisory Group, comprising Steven Tallman, Bain's former vice president of training, and five senior partners; the Bain Virtual University, an online multimedia learning network formed in 1998; and Bain's Global Experience Center (GCX), the core of Bain's intranet-based knowledge management system, which taps the collective expertise of Bain consultants worldwide.

8. *Learning should support and be supported by Bain's "outside-in" approach to solving business problems.* As Tierney explains: "You need to look *outside* a company and even outside the client's industry for new insights. Tierney envisions creating an academy of best-of-Bain thinkers to search for, digest, and interpret relevant business insights. These insights could then be applied in Bain consulting assignments and in Bain Training & Development programs.

Buckman Laboratories: Building a Knowledge Sharing Network

A specialty chemical company with operations in over 21 countries and customers in more than 90 countries, Buckman Laboratories several years ago found itself in an uncomfortable position: its business worldwide was growing by leaps and bounds. But the privately-owned company's centralized "command and control" style of management forced sales representatives to refer critical decisions to company headquarters in Memphis, Tennessee. Delays in handling customer inquiries were beginning to take their toll on customer service—and future sales growth.

Worse still, it was becoming impractical to train, educate, and update all global associates on every development within the company on a face-to-face basis. The specialty paper industry, a core business at Buckman Laboratories, was experiencing rapid growth in the use of new technologies. Classroom training for a global sales force was no longer feasible in this environment. Years ago company founder Stanley Buckman could carry the company's collective wisdom around in his head, but it was becoming impossible for any one person to retain all the information, and pass it on to the field sales force. Better training methods had to be found.

Dr. Bob Buckman, Stanley Buckman's son and current CEO, understood the importance of free exchange of information, supported by training, shortly after taking office. "We recognize that we are not only providing products and services to our customers—we are delivering knowledge and expertise," he says. Bob Buckman's vision of the company's purpose stems from his commitment to creative problem solving for the customer. In the early 1980s, before most of the world had heard of the Internet, Bob Buckman began trying to establish international networks for electronic communications.

Buckman's Education Benefit

One benefit Buckman Laboratories offers both its associates and their dependents reveals the value its CEO places on continued learning and education. Since Bob Buckman's takeover of the company in the 70s, every Buckman associate (employee) has the ability to pursue his or her higher education, to any level, in any field of expertise, at the company's expense. Buckman pays full benefits for all expenses associated with further education, from any university, local or otherwise, for a BA/BS, MA/MS, and Ph.D. In the late 90s, on-line universities have been added through the Buckman Learning Center so that individuals can take courses more easily than ever through using the laptop computer every Buckman associate carries at all times. Associates can request, and often receive, sabbaticals from their jobs to attend universities at locations away from Memphis, Tennessee, the corporate headquarters.

Such importance placed on higher education encourages every associate to strive to be the best and most currently educated he or she can be. Needless to say, the education benefits at Buckman have translated into an employee population with a high regard for knowledge and information and extremely high levels of employee loyalty. Also, every employee at Buckman is encouraged to complete the highest level of college education he or she desires. (This all ties into Buckman's Learning Culture.) Another tie-in is the fact that Buckman has never laid off any employees. If their talent and expertise are no longer specifically needed by the company, work of some kind will be offered to the associate in another part of the company.

C 2001, Courtesy of Buckman Laboratories

Bob Buckman's vision of enhanced communications between associates all over the world led to the creation of his most important "product"—the earliest and best broad-scale knowledge sharing capability in the specialty chemical industry, K'Netix®, the Buckman Knowledge Network. The network was designed to realize Buckman's vision of bringing to bear the total knowledge of the worldwide company in solving any customer business or process challenge. With K'Netix, the ideas and solutions of one person or group can be rapidly shared with associates anywhere in the world. Today, response to customer needs must be as fast as technology allows and as accurate as the collective knowledge the company can provide.

How did Buckman's journey begin? In the mid- through latter 80s, he had a series of conversations with Dick Ross, retired vice president of marketing, and one of the founder's most trusted advisors. Buckman wanted to develop a more efficient and timely way in which to train and inform Buckman associates worldwide. The old way, sending specialists (like Dr. Ross) sprinting from country to country, spreading the latest news and gathering the latest information was not expedient any longer.

It took too much time to send someone around the world to gather news, and it did not empower the individual associate with the tools he needed to request information and to disseminate his own reports. The first germ of an idea for knowledge management architecture sprang from these discussions, which took place in the early 1980s. Early in the process, as requests for information came in from the field, some associates were used as "runners." They would identify those who could best answer requests, take requests to them, and prod them to answer. The runners would take down the answers and transmit them by fax or phone to the requestor. This worked well for a beginning step but the process was paper-based and slow—sometimes requiring weeks to process and return.

As Bob Buckman had realized, 86 percent of Buckman Laboratories more than 1,200 employees are out of the office at any given time, working with customers located in more than 90 countries. This diverse and dispersed workforce presents special problems for the creation and management of the company's intellectual capital. Faced with these challenges and the need to bring new knowledge and skills to its employees in a cost-effective manner, Buckman Laboratories has created an on-line, multi-lingual learning center. Its goal is to create a learning center for delivering and facilitating world-class training and educational opportunities, *when and where the employees need them.*

The CEO's Involvement in Employee Learning

Buckman is continually looking for new windows of opportunity to support the front-line workers, the ones who interface with the customers daily. Bob Buckman says, "If we can give them unlimited power to close the gap with the customer—*unlimited power*—then nobody can beat them in solving problems for the customer. The customers want results—they don't care how we get them—they just want results as fast as possible."

The sales force is generally not in the office and often has little support in the field. In fact, technical sales representatives are usually out alone in the field. They need and want to support increased profit, quality, and product for their customers. Knowledge management really comes down to getting more and more power to meet the needs of the customer through the salesman. K'Netix enables the sales-technical rep to call on the rest of the organization for information instead of the rest of the organization telling him what to do. This creates a shift from a product-driven organization to a completely market-driven organization. What's the key to implementing knowledge management? Empower the worker. Knowledge management is all about supporting front-line workers with the knowledge they need to help the customer.

Virtual Learning Takes Hold at Buckman Labs

The Buckman Learning Center is the latest innovation in the K'Netix infrastructure designed to cost effectively provide associates the learning they require when and where they need it. The Learning Center was founded in 1997 with two basic strategic assumptions. First, Buckman's competitive advantage resides in the collective knowledge of its associates. Second, in order to sustain that advantage, Buckman Laboratories must steward the professional development of associates by investing in the growth of their skills and competencies.

To meet this challenge, the Learning Center delivers 24/7 access to the company's learning and training opportunities. Through the Learning Center's website, associates can review their progress against their training and development plans, access over 600 on-line courses ranging from water chemistry to personal productivity to budgeting and planning, register for any of the company's regularly scheduled instructor lead courses, or pursue an on-line degree program. Supervisors can create group-training plans, review their associates' training histories, perform skills gap analysis on associates and teams, and create training budgets.

C 2001, Courtesy of Buckman Laboratories

Stemming from the discussions between Richard T. Ross and Bob Buckman in the late 1980s about how to connect employees globally, Buckman Laboratories embarked on a journey to tie its associates together electronically in a virtual community. Today, K'Netix allows associates to participate in virtual discussion groups around the flow of industry-specific and general company information.

This diverse and dispersed workforce presents barriers to the creation and management of the company's knowledge base and intellectual capital. The transfer of information often occurs over great distances and time.

In many cases Buckman's virtual university provides cost-effective alternatives to traditional instructor-led events. Virtual learning centers increase the value of face-to-face learning events by shifting the more rudimentary learning to a self-paced module the learner completes before attending class. Technology also shifts the synchronous classroom to the virtual world. Learning activities are delivered synchronously through video conferencing or via the computer desktop. Other content is delivered as self-paced modules (Web- or computer-based training) or asynchronous instructor-facilitated learning events

The Buckman Learning Center has demonstrated considerable cost savings over many traditional training methods. In one study, utilizing the tools of the Buckman Learning Center resulted in cost savings of 50 percent over what would have been the costs of offering the training through traditional means.

There are other savings for the company as well: travel cost to the classroom is eliminated, housing cost at the site where the education is conducted is eliminated. The classroom is blended with technology. All of this allows the company to use learning funds more effectively. [4]

BUCKMAN LEARNING CENTER UNDER-THE-HOOD:

- **Learning Management System:** click2learn.com's Ingenium
- **Partnerships:** FranklinCovey, DigitalThink, NETg, University of Phoenix, Western Michigan University, and the Institute of Paper Science and Technology.
- **Translation Programs:** Systrans (e-dictionary) and Trados (sentence memory) blended with human translator

Source: Buckman Laboratories

Dell Computer Corporation:
Training a Hypergrowth Workforce

The world's largest direct seller of personal computers, Dell Computer credits its stunning success to the integration of employee training and Dell's strategy of selling directly to end-users. Training had always been a part of Dell's strategy. By 1995, however, it was clear that employee training needed an even greater emphasis. That year Dell's Office of the Chairman directed that the role of Dell Learning be significantly expanded. The charter of the (then) corporate university was relatively simple but incredibly challenging: ensuring that people had the knowledge and skills to keep pace with the hypergrowth of the company—annual sales growth of 30% a year. At the time Dell was adding—or "onboarding"—as many as 200 to 300 new employees every week.

A news article appearing in the *Wall Street Journal* titled "Dell or be Delled" seemed to sum up the company's intense drive to be the number one supplier in the PC industry. Being "Delled" was described as having your business taken away by someone who leaps ahead of you and fundamentally changes the rules of your business. Dell understood that threat and realized its success as a business would depend on how fast it could learn what's next, and apply what it learns to the service of its customers.

One could easily assume that Michael Dell, the founder of this multi-billion dollar company in his college dorm room, had a fully formed vision of his training organization from the start. For Dell Computer Corporation, the visionary role of this CEO has always been one of seeing a future that others don't (yet); setting a bold direction; naming a target (usually one that appears unreachable to most everyone else); and outlining the critical few criteria that must be met in reaching that target. This can also be said about Michael Dell's role as visionary for education. He sets the targets and then demands that the training organization deliver the results.

At a very practical level, Michael Dell's vision of training is synchronous with his vision of the business. What he asked for is a training function that has speed, can scale with a company in hypergrowth, uses technology, and is direct. That last criterion, the basis of the company business model, is the most important.

Dell Learning, responsible for all education in the company, was given four key objectives:

1. Align learning with key business initiatives.
2. Make learning directly available to everyone who needs it.
3. Create clarity around competencies required for continued success.
4. Provide consistency, where needed, through global curricula.

In response to the hypergrowth of the company, three-quarters of the training provided was aimed at new hires, training on company products and services, and basic job skills. This was the trigger for the organization and the first initiative Dell Learning focused on in imp[lamenting its new vision.

To meet that charter, a centralized corporate team was formed to establish processes for training development and administration. Training managers, reporting directly into each business or function, were appointed to perform four key tasks:

a. Developing a business-based education plan
b. Holding the business leaders responsible for execution of the plan
c. Ensuring that the resources exist to successfully execute the plan
d. Reporting to the business on the impact of that plan

In addition to providing strategic direction, the corporate team also includes fulfillment teams that serve the businesses on demand. One team produces learning tools so that the businesses can train sales and technical audiences on Dell's products and services. Another, Education Services, manages classrooms, registration, scheduling, tracking, and a number of other logistical aspects of training. A third group consists of highly experienced instructional designers who oversee development projects requested by the businesses. Because of the critical importance of the shift to technology, the Dell Learning Technology Services group was added to the corporate training organization in 1999 focused exclusively on enabling the use of technology and nontraditional training methods. Dell Learning has a goal to move as much as 90 percent of formal learning out of the classroom.

The Dell Philosophy of Education

Essentially, the Dell training organization operates as a federation. There are three component parts: Corporate Training, Regional (HR) Training, and Regional (Non-HR) Training. The federation is held together by the senior management team and by a series of Dell Learning Councils. This organizational structure was, in part, a response to an even greater expansion of the charter for training at Dell. At about the time that the "university" designation was dropped (it was seen as too limiting and was replaced with the name "Dell Learning") the charter was revised to include 10 principles:

1. Education should be business-issue based.

2. Education should be as cost effective and time effective as possible.

3. The business manager should be in charge of managing her/his training investments.

4. Education must be very flexible and able to scale.

5. All training should be competency based.

6. All learning should be "just enough just in time."

7. Learners should be in control of their own development.

8. Learning solutions have limited shelf life and should be treated accordingly.

9. Learning occurs everywhere, so our obligation is to leverage it across the organization.

10. The education function must create access to the intellectual capital of Dell.

Company Founder Michael Dell sums the Dell philosophy of training this way:

"Our industry is constantly changing with the rapid evolution of technology. Our business model is unique, unlike any other company. In addition we continue to grow at 2-3 times the rate of our industry. All of these factors combine to place a huge priority in our company in education and training. Without a strong understanding of our unique business model and the strategies of our company, our performance would be about like all the companies that have been unsuccessful in competing with us. Everyone has to be open to learning all the time, starting with me and everyone must support and encourage their teams to make sure they have the knowledge and skills to succeed."

c 2001, courtesy of Dell Computer Corporation.

Michael Dell also understood the importance of personal connections. From the very early days of the company, Michael insisted on holding semi-annual executive conferences. When asked why, he explained that the fundamental purpose for the meetings was relationship building. "We operate in different time zones. Much of what we do together will have to be handled through technology—e-mail, phone, the Internet. Having personal relationships makes using that technology easier."

Finally, however, the vision for learning at Dell is subordinate to the vision for the business. Michael Dell closed his presentation to the last executive conference by outlining the top five things that each vice president in the company had to do in the coming year. "First and foremost," he said, "hiring and developing new talent remains essential for us to execute the strategic and organizational vision we have outlined."

The business benefits from Dell's emphasis on learning may be obvious. What may be more important is something much subtler. Learning is a part of how Dell Computer Corporation does business. The visible example of the CEO is comparable to his involvement in the financial management of the company or its technology roadmap.

Dell Computer, like it's founder, is still young. It hasn't had the time to develop decades of tradition and experience. Those involved at Dell will candidly admit that there is much more that they could be doing; much more that they want to do. But the company learns quickly and so do the people in it—and the desire to keep learning starts at the top.[5]

General Electric's Learning Culture

Jack Welch, the chairman and CEO of General Electric, has managed during his long tenure a financial turnaround of General Electric, and helped earn GE the title of "most respected company in America" according to Fortune magazine. Perhaps more significantly, Welch has engineered a cultural transformation within General Electric.

One of Welch's first actions when he assumed the title of CEO in 1981 was to eliminate layers of middle management through a series of highly unpopular layoffs, or what he called "getting rid of the layers" and creating an informal, open organization. Today, all GE business units report directly to the CEO's office, consisting of Welch and two vice chairmen.

In his speeches to GE employees, Welch often talked about creating a "learning culture" and a "learning organization" within GE. Welch reasoned that GE managers would gain competitive advantage by openly sharing ideas and learning from each other. Welch encouraged open discussion, and learning, at meetings of GE's senior executives in which he routinely quizzed GE's top managers, telling them it was all right if they didn't have an answer to one of his questions. (Welch called these open-ended discussions "boundaryless meetings.") "That's okay," he would say. "Just make sure you find out the answer and let me know what it is."

Perhaps the best indication of whether CEOs do their job as a Chief Education Officer is whether senior leaders at the company tapped to go on and lead other companies. This has certainly been the case at General Electric where many talented business managers have gone on to become Chief Executive Officers at other large companies. A list of Former General Electric Executives is listed below.

Former General Electric Executive	Company
Bruce R. Albertson	Iomega
Stephen M. Bennett	Intuit
John B. Blystone	SPX
Stanley C. Gault	Goodyear
Glen H. Hilner	Owens Corning
Thomas S. Rogers	Primedia
Thomas C. Tiller	Polaris Industries
John M. Trani	Stanley Works
Gary C. Wendt	Conseco

Figure 2-1 Source: The New York Times 11/29/00

In the GE business model, managers get together and share ideas about what works, and what doesn't, in their respective businesses. All GE businesses report directly to the CEO and two vice chairmen. A cornerstone of the Boundaryless Company is something that GE calls "Work-Out," which literally means that everyone in the company can express their opinion if they have something to say. The GE Workout program is a multistep process, starting with "town meetings" involving small groups of employees, expanding later on to include GE customers.

GE's business managers are also encouraged to benchmark best practices and borrow ideas if an idea can be shown to have merit. GE became a corporate advocate of Six Sigma quality control, following the example set by Motorola. It also learned effective sourcing and supply chain management from General Motors and Toyota, and product integration from Chrysler and Canon. It was Jack Welch's vision of a global company that led to GE's expansion into international markets in 1987, and its expansion into business services. GE's business services, led by its GE Capital subsidiary, today account for more than 75% of revenues, versus only 15% of revenues in 1980.

Welch credits GE's learning culture for several improvements in the company's financial performance, including higher operating margins and improved company earnings. GE earnings, after showing single digit increases through the 1980s, have been growing at double-digit levels annually since 1992.[6]

Take the GE Learning Culture Test

1. Do you find that senior managers in your company have little sympathy for ideas they did not come up with?
   Yes   No

2. Do you personally feel that there is little to learn from the other parts of your business?
   Yes   No

3. Have you made a conscious effort in the last year to pick the brains of other colleagues to find out what they know that might be applied in your own work?
   Yes   No

4. Do you automatically assume that the way you and your company have been doing things is the best way, and there's no point in trying to learn what others are doing?
   Yes   No

5. Does your company offer any opportunity, formal or informal, for various divisions to share ideas?
   Yes   No

If you answered two or more of these questions in the affirmative, it is likely that you are part of the old way of doing business, and that there is much to learn from GE's attitude toward the need for a true learning culture within a business.

Source: *Jack Welch's Battle Plan for Corporate Revolution: The GE Way Fieldbook*

Memorial Hermann Healthcare System: Partner in Caring

Spending on health care services, including hospital and physician care, totals $1.4 trillion in annual spending, making it the largest industry in the U.S., and also the largest employer. Memorial Hermann Healthcare

System, a 12-hospital system based in Houston, Texas, is one of the largest health care systems in the United States. Dan S. Wilford, CEO of Memorial Hermann since 1984, has been a visionary in guiding Memorial Hermann through some difficult years financially. Memorial Hermann, like other hospital centers, was hit hard by the 1997 Balanced Budget Act, which substantially reduced federal Medicare payments to hospitals.

Wilford credits Memorial Hermann's Partners in Caring program, a program he helped initiate, for contributing to the success of a financial turnaround following the change in Medicare funding. Following a very poor year in 1999, Memorial Hermann regained profitability in 2000, a $100-million financial turnaround in a little more than a year—a remarkable recovery for a nonprofit healthcare system. Wilford strongly believes this achievement would not have been possible without the Partners in Caring Program and the high level of training given Memorial employees.[7]

Partners in Caring was initiated in 1988 when Wilford appointed 10 employees and challenged them to "create a unique environment where all who enter our doors would feel they were someplace special." Those employees answered the challenge, and proposed that Memorial employees create that unique environment. The Partners in Caring program sets levels of behavioral expectation—there are 36 behavioral expectations in all—that Memorial Herman's 13,400 employees are expected to achieve. Employees failing to meet these job performance goals (See Figure 2-2) are given counseling to improve their job performance skills. An indicator of its success is modeling by other hospital systems; more than 20 hospital systems have used the Memorial Hermann behavioral expectations for benchmarking and employee training.

Figure 2-2 Behavioral Expectations at Memorial Hermann

As Partners in Caring, it is our responsibility to treat all our customers, including patients, families, physicians, co-workers and all outside contacts with courtesy, dignity, respect and professionalism. The following is an assessment of your performance relative to each of those behavioral expectations.

Assessment Rating: 3 = Exceeds Expectations   2 = Meets Expectations
                         1 = Does Not Meet Expectations

Any '3' Rating Requires A Written Example. With certain of the behaviors, you either do or don't meet expectations and therefore are rated as either a "1" or "2".

EXPECTATIONS	Circle the Appropriate Rating
COURTESY	
• **Welcomes and/or greets internal and external customers in a professional, polite and respectful way.**	1 or 2 or 3
• **Greets others in hallways, elevators and at workstations with a kind word or smile.**	1 or 2 or 3
• **Assists people in finding proper resources for problem resolution.**	1 or 2 or 3
■ **Assists customers in finding their way.**	1 or 2 or 3
• **Makes eye contact; introduces self and explains purpose, when appropriate.**	1 or 2 or 3
• **Listens carefully; does not interrupt; gives people full attention.**	1 or 2 or 3

RESPECT	
• **Respects privacy and dignity.**	1 or 2
• **Uses a professional and respectful tone of voice.**	1 or 2
• **Discusses confidential or sensitive information about customers, employees, or hospital business only with those having a valid need to know, and does so privately, never in public places.**	1 or 2
	1 or 2
• **Does not make disparaging remarks about others.**	
	1 or 2
• **Respects individual and cultural differences.**	
RESPONSIVENESS	
• **Responds in a timely manner to requests for help.**	1 or 2 or 3
• **Provides the services or information requested, or finds someone who can.**	1 or 2 or 3
	1 or 2 or 3
• **Provides a timeframe for providing services and explains any delays.**	
COMMUNICATION	
• **Offers information on departmental processes and procedures, as appropriate.**	1 or 2 or 3
	1 or 2 or 3
• **Invites questions and comments.**	
	1 or 2 or 3
• **Communicates with clarity and professionalism both orally and in writing.**	
	1 or 2 or 3
• **Keeps people informed while resolving issues or getting answers to questions.**	
	1 or 2 or 3
• **Speaks English or the language of the person being helped. Arranges for interpretation services when needed.**	

<u>TEAMWORK</u>	
• **Takes responsibility for improving processes and systems; looks for new and better ways of doing things.**	1 or 2 or 3
• **Works as a member of the Memorial Hermann Healthcare System team; performs duties in a way that makes it easier for others to perform theirs.**	1 or 2 or 3
• **Follows through in meeting deadlines and keeping promises.**	1 or 2 or 3
	1 or 2 or 3
• **Works with customers and clients to address complaints, frustrations and service problems.**	1 or 2 or 3
• **Participates openly, honestly shares opinions, and looks for new and better ways of doing things.**	1 or 2 or 3
• **Maintains positive working relationships with co -workers and customers.**	1 or 2 or 3
• **Demonstrates willingness to accept assignments in a positive manner.**	
<u>PROFESSIONALISM</u>	
• **Presents a positive image.**	1 or 2 or 3
• **Wears name badge or nametag so that name is clearly visible at all times while on duty.**	1 or 2
• **Limits eating, drinking and smoking to designated areas.**	1 or 2
• **Avoids personal conversations with co -workers when providing patient care or other customer service.**	1 or 2
• **Makes no inappropriate or negative comment about patients, co -workers, physicians or any part of Memorial Hermann Healthcare System in the presence or within the hearing of any internal or external customer.**	1 or 2

• **Demonstrates pride in Memorial Hermann Healthcare System by keeping areas clean and safe.**	1 or 2 or 3
• **Demonstrates a professional attitude toward co-workers and customers.**	1 or 2 or 3
• **Demonstrates an ongoing responsibility and commitment to the job through attendance and punctuality in relation to stated work hours.**	1 or 2 or 3
• **Follows appropriate telephone guidelines.**	1 or 2 or 3
• **Maintains professional appearance and manner that is appropriate to assignment, as well as following Memorial Hermann Healthcare Systems Appearance Standard Guidelines.**	1 or 2
Behavioral Expectations Assessment Total Points	
Average Assessment (divided by 36) =	

Source: Memorial Hermann Healthcare System

Memorial Hermann employees must achieve a minimum average score of **1.88** to be eligible for an annual merit increase.

Wilford—the co-author of a book on health care management—places a high degree of trust in his employees. A shortage of skilled employees, especially nurses, has its impact on quality of patient care. Wilford tackled that issue by naming each Memorial supservisor "chief retention officer" in the unit under their supervision, and the strategy is beginning to achieve results. A favorite Wilford measure of the amount of trust in each employee is something he calls the "Trust Dimension." Each Memorial employee, according to this model, can do 95% of the work done by employees they supervise. The difference (5%) is the part of an employee's job that only they can do. The organization has to trust them to do it. That is the Trust Dimension. (See Figure 2-3).

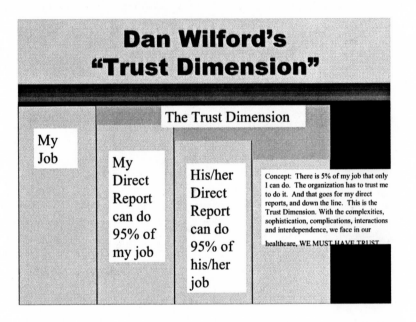

Figure 2-3: The Trust Dimension

Chapter Summary

A number of success factors contribute in the design and launch of an enterprise-wide learning initiative or a corporate university. By far, the most critical success factor is the personal role of the CEO. A survey of more than 100 corporate university deans by Corporate University Xchange indicates one common theme—the CEOs at companies with world-class corporate universities spend a considerable amount of time cultivating and managing the culture and intellectual capital of their organizations.

CEOs contribute to the success of their learning initiatives by:

1. Functioning as Chief Education Officer—cultivating and developing leaders throughout the organization.

2. Crystallizing the learning philosophy of the organization.

3. Identifying learning goals for all employees.

4. Enlisting the support of senior business managers.

5. Publicly acknowledging the importance of life-long learning.

6. Encouraging experimenting with new forms of learning.

Action Steps: Getting CEO Support

1. Focus on the triggers of the organization. Identify the "burning issues" these triggers are having in your organization. These may include:

   • Increasing new employee productivity

   • Retaining the best workforce

   • Building the next generation of leadership

2. Gain credibility by starting to show results fast. Cycle time is just as important in learning as it is in manufacturing.

3. Showcase successes. Make stars out of the leaders who are teachers.

4. Create incentives and rewards to everyone involved in the organization's learning vision.

5. Identify champions and ignore nay sayers. They will eventually get on board.

6. Develop a task force representing all parts of the organization; you have to share the vision of learning, involving all sectors.

7. Learning, above all else, must support specific, quantitative business objectives. If it doesn't, you are unlikely to get support and funding from the CEO.

Lesson #2

Identify and communicate how
an education investment achieves business goals

CHAPTER THREE:

▼

THE CEO AS SPONSOR

"We want to have the best educated workforce on the planet."
—*George David, CEO, United Technologies Corporation*

The question for CEOs continues to be "How do you enhance learning through out the organization? [1] This question has taken on new importance as CEOs are faced with the challenge of having their global workforce reflect a single set of values and one company vision. In Jeffrey Garten's book, *The Mind of the CEO*, Jack Welch comments on why CEOs are particularly interested in figuring out how to inculcate a common vision to all employees: "Leadership of companies is going to become much less CEO-driven. People within the company are going to have so much data on their hands that they will be able to challenge a CEO's decisions all the time. The pace of events is going to be so fast that people aren't going to wait for the next layer of management approvals. There's going to have to be much more delegation and participation. The leader much become an ever more engaging coach. You are going to have to create an environment where excitement reigns where challenges are everywhere and where the rewards are both in the wallet and in the soul." [2]

The CEO, by providing encouragement, resources and commitment for strategic learning, builds support for new learning programs and the education practice throughout the organization. This may be the most common role for the CEO of any organization. Some high-profile CEOs, such as GE's Jack Welch and Bob Buckman of Buckman Laboratories, are passionate advocates for lifelong learning and continuous career development.

As sponsors of enterprise-wide learning, CEOs deliver more than vocal support. They provide funding for new learning initiatives. They meet with learning advisory council members, including the Chief Learning Officer, and help set goals for learning programs. They set an example for business unit managers. CEO sponsorship can take place in a variety of forms:

- Participation in Leadership Development Programs
- Initiation of academic partnerships with colleges and universities
- Introduction of new enterprise-wide learning programs such as e-learning
- Adapting learning activities to support a new business model

CEO sponsorship in most, if not all, of these learning ventures extends well beyond an appearance in the obligatory company video telling why this or that initiative is important, or the chief executive's message on the first page of a training catalog reminding employees of the obligation to learn. CEO sponsorship for learning is an active involvement rather than just a public commitment t6o life-long learning

Dell Computer: A Learning Strategy in Transition

At Dell Computer, CEO Michael Dell is personally involved in helping develop new and innovative learning programs. When his company decided to move aggressively into e-business, Michael Dell commissioned the creation of "Know the Net." This on-line training module teaches the company's Internet strategy, sets expectations for all employees, and shows them how to use the Internet themselves. It includes a test so they can prove they "Know the Net."

Michael Dell launched the new program personally, with e-mail communications and repeated references at staff meetings and company forums. Instead of traditional course completion certificates, anyone who passed the test received a certificate with a picture of the CEO and the note, "Michael Says I Know The Net." As he went from meeting to meeting, the youthful CEO personally checked for the certificates. (It should be no surprise that the company has now transitioned to automatically generated "e-certificates" that employees can choose to print, use as screensavers, or transfer to a file.) He insisted on regular updates on the percentages of people successfully completing the training. Says Dell, "The Internet is crucial to our future. Every one of us needs to understand it and the power it brings to the company. When learning is this important to the business, it's everybody's job to get behind it—especially mine."

Similarly, when the company's ethics committee teamed with Dell Learning to create a series of programs for managers on key issues such as preventing sexual harassment and the Dell Code of Conduct, all managers were required to attend them. Michael Dell asked to be personally notified about compliance with the 100% attendance goal. He sent letters of congratulations to managers whose organizations were hitting the targets and some very pointed messages to those who were not. His personal involvement as sponsor was clear.

Dell also sponsors the previously mentioned annual vice presidents conference at his company, together with Vice Chairmen Mort Topfer and Kevin Rollins (and now with new Vice Chairman, Jim Vanderslice.) This global event aims at strengthening the relationships within the leadership team, creating consistent approaches to company issues, and fundamentally building leadership knowledge and skills.

The members of the chairman's office select a theme for each event; plan the agenda; select outside speakers; and in addition to making presentations, they often facilitate or manage learning activities that are part of the program. Programs are wide ranging. Past programs have focused on building a culture of commitment, launching Dell's Internet strategy, improving the customer experience, and leading rapid change. The commitment to the conference is personal. In past years the program has included dinner at the CEOs home. At Dell's direction, the company's major regions hold similar programs annually as well, with attendance extended to the director level.

According to John Coné, President of Dell Learning, Michael Dell's sponsorship of the "Customer Experience" initiative went far beyond a commitment to learning. It began when the chairman's office commissioned the start of QUEST training in the company. QUEST stands for Quality Underlies Every Single Task. The top execs at Dell personally drove the initiative to provide quality tools to every employee. They personally managed the evolution of the program from its initial focus on internal quality standards to the current external approach of creating the best possible customer experience. [3]

The CEO's sponsorship also includes strategic funding for special programs. Most often, the funding supports broad areas like diversity education or ethics and values, but sometimes the sponsorships are more directed. When, on a recent visit to one of the company's regions, Michael Dell discovered the need for more training on Dell's new products, he asked one of the vice chairmen, Mort Topfer, to take a personal interest in fixing the problem. Over the next 30 days, top executives spent hours working on the issue with the regional management team and Dell Learning. The result was a strategic appropriation to make sure that the training happened, an extensive project plan to make certain that the right things would be done, and a clear commitment from the entire management team to support the plan.

There's another, more subtle kind of sponsorship of learning at Dell, one that is a reflection of the company itself and the changes it is making to the way businesses work. Michael Dell believes that everyone in his company deserves access to e-tools that will help them do their jobs. Call it technology-based learning, call it performance support, or just call it (as Dell does) tools to help you succeed. Dell Computer Corporation is committed to providing an environment that encourages and supports learning—directly. For example, anyone accessing the company's internal website will see an icon called "Manager Tools." Clicking there, over 50 options appear, including tools for compensation planning, team and self development, hiring and assimilating new employees, and performance management.

One of the guiding principles at Dell Learning is that employees must have control over their own learning, whenever and wherever they want to access a training course (see Figure 2-1). These principles and the direct nature of the computer business have required the company to move aggressively toward technology-enabled learning. Today, more than half of all formal learning at Dell takes place outside of the classroom. (Dell Learning delivers training in a range of multi-media formats, including CD-ROM and web-based formats.) If the learner is really going to be in control, then the learning solution has to be available twenty four hours a day, seven days a week. Dell Learning has a goal to move as much as 90 percent of formal learning out of the classroom.

The individual controls what she or he will learn, when the learning starts and stops, if it's interrupted, and what elements it includes. Sometimes, low-tech solutions can make this possible. Classroom learning never can. Technology can make learning solutions ubiquitous and a very natural part of work. It's worth noting that, although individuals are in charge of their learning, they don't make decisions in a vacuum. The performance planning process at Dell requires people to create development plans that are supported (and sponsored) by their managers. Dell Learning's registration system automatically notifies managers of developmental actions and gives them the option to approve those actions.

Examples of Dell Computer's sponsorship (and Michael Dell's personal involvement as a sponsoring CEO) of enterprise-wide learning are myriad, and can be found throughout the company. New Dell employees receive a thorough introduction to the Dell Business Model, the company's direct-to-end-user sales model, eliminating the use of distributors, resellers and emphasizing Dell's market niche—made-to-order PC's at competitive prices.

Learning at Dell is based on the needs of the business. So Dell Learning creates curriculum "roadmaps" and self-assessments. Based on the skills and knowledge needed to succeed in particular jobs, roadmaps depict a logical sequence of learning. The assessments, most of them on-line, allow the individual to determine the gaps between his current abilities and what's on the roadmap. In that way, each individual can customize his development. Today, roadmaps include Management & Executive Education, Sales, Marketing, Finance, a number of technical certifications, and Information Technology, to name a few.

An example in the sales area is the Dell Education Roadmap depicted in Figure 3-1.

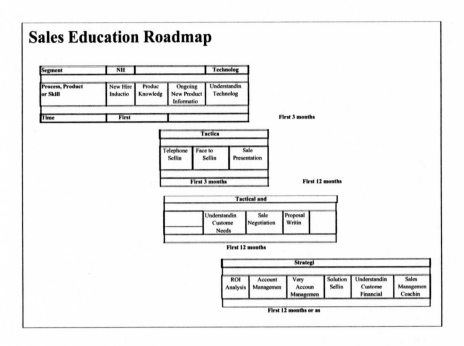

Figure 3-1

If you talk to any of the Dell Learning team, they are likely to tell you that the most important change to make is the most fundamental: really put the learner in charge. Most training departments, they will tell you, have a vested interest in an older paradigm. After all, the training department is typically the intermediary between the company and the individual when it comes to learning. It organizes content, designs programs, creates class schedules, and teaches the classes or selects the instructors. What can develop from that responsibility is a tendency to believe that employees can't learn without all of that support. At Dell Learning, John Coné refers to this legacy as the "children with chainsaws" principle—as Coné says, "It's the idea that letting people manage their own learning is as dangerous as giving a running chainsaw to a seven-year-old."

And there are measurable returns. Dell's investment in learning has paid off in cost avoidance, increased sales, improvements in employee productivity, and better customer service. It has even helped recruiting, as employees concerned with development cite it as reason for deciding to join the company. At a more subtle level too, the company has been able to keep up its phenomenal growth and maintain consistency of message and focus in key areas.

Once CEOs are involved as Sponsors, they want reports on the effectiveness of their investment in learning. So it is the job of the training department to create a measurement system that provides on-line access for senior managers, including the CEO, to training statistics at global, business, segment, and departmental levels. Dell Learning developed Four key reports available online so Dell Managers could monitor where and how their investment in learning was being spent. These are:

- *Training Snapshot Report.* This report documents all training activity including classes taken; total tuition; total enrollment; total hours by region, business and segment.

- *Training by Type.* This report sorts training activity by category, such as Management, Executive, Customer Service, Sales, New Product Sales, New Product Technical, New Hire, Business Initiatives, Professional Development, and Compliance.

- *CBT/On-line Training Report.* This report documents all computer-based training and on-line training completed for the fiscal year.

- *Customer Satisfaction Report.* This report is a summary of all training evaluations completed and submitted by course.

In the past two years a total of nine return-on-investment studies on the training in sales, procurement, new hire, new product, and software were completed. The results showed additional revenues and cost savings of approximately $75 million to various Dell business units. These ROI results were then wed to reinforce and sustain improvement in performance. Dell Learning utilized analysis results to design new product performance support system tools. These tools integrate with the Dell universal sales process.

At the direction of its leaders, Dell Computer Corporation has created a working environment where learning is always available right away. As vice chairman Mort Topfer says: "Learning is key to Dell's continued success. The focus and need for continuing education must come from the top. We need, and will have, strong leadership from the CEO's office."

Deutsche Bank:
The Spokesman's Challenge
and a New Generation of Banking Leadership

As one of the world's leading financial institutions, Deutsche Bank has both a long history and a stake in defining the shape and scope of banking in the 21st century. Founded in 1870, Deutsche Bank has grown through acquisition in recent years, acquiring British merchant bank Morgan Grenfell in 1989 and New York-based Bankers Trust Company in 1997.

Rolf-E Breuer, who holds the title of CEO (or Spokesman of the Executive Board, a title conferred by German law), has been Deutsche Bank's chief executive since 1997. In 1998, Breuer led Deutsche Bank through a major reorganization. He realized that Deutsche Bank had to transform itself into a multi-specialist financial services provider whose individual business lines successfully compete with the best specialists in their respective market segments.

"We were not focused enough," Breuer explains, "and many analysts believed we were cross-subsidizing not-so-profitable businesses with the more profitable ones. My answer to that is: we restructured the bank into divisions, and the private banking division, for instance, is competing with the best private banks and is not subsidized by somebody else. And the asset manager is competing with the best asset managers in the world and is not cross-subsidized."

Today, Deutsche Bank is structured as a virtual holding company with a lean Corporate Center and the following five core business units:

1. Global Corporates and Institutions (GCI), serving the two thousand largest institutional and corporate clients. GCI is comparable to a U.S. type of investment bank providing both advisory and trading services.

2. Global Technology and Services (GTS), developing and maintaining Deutsche Bank's IT services and infrastructure as well as providing financial transaction services to both internal and external customers.

3. Asset Management (AM), providing both institutional as well as private and retail asset management products.

4. Corporate and Real Estate (CORE), serving mid-sized and large corporate customers.

5. Retail and Private Banking (UBP), serving the traditional retail client base in Germany, Spain, and Italy, as well as high net-worth individuals around the globe.

The new structure enabled Deutsche Bank to pursue a "dual focus" strategy. The bank intends to capitalize on the opportunities offered by both the new Euro capital markets as well as the new business that a "deregulated" European marketplace will continue to generate. Deutsche Bank is also well positioned to capitalize on the continuing globalization of the financial services industry by aggressively expanding its activities in non-European markets.

Deutsche Bank's divisional restructuring, splitting the company into business units organized by line of business, soon led to a re-examination of its staff development and staff training functions. Deutsche Bank has always been very concerned with the development of its staff and has traditionally invested a considerable amount of its revenues—on average more than four percent of net income—in the training and education of its employees. In fact, this attitude has long been an important part of the bank and Germany's culture.

Aligning Training with Business Activities

Deutsche Bank is committed to redefining its learning function in order to combine individual learning and development more effectively with the learning and development of the organization. The new learning function aims at helping Deutsche Bank successfully compete in the knowledge-based society of the twenty-first century.

In investment banking, training and development is critically important due to the fast-moving nature of the capital markets. The name of the game is knowledge and how it is used to offer our customers value-added solutions. Unless employees are constantly learning and keeping pace with market developments a company cannot add value to their customers, they don't make money and do not create shareholder value. Deutsche Bank sees learning as key in this environment in order to be successful.

Traditionally, Deutsche Bank developed the managerial competencies of its executives "naturally" through successive job assignments, or off the job, by sending them to open-enrollment executive education programs at leading business schools and executive education centers worldwide. This approach was quite appropriate in the past when the corporate culture of the bank was very homogeneous. However, it was no longer sufficient or desirable in the light of the increasing globalization and divisionalization of the firm in the 21st century. Today, more than half of the Deutsche Bank staff work abroad and in three divisions the non-German employees are in the majority.

As Michael Maffucci of Deutsche Bank says: "The staff at Deutsche Bank is multicultural and we are all engaged in a diverse variety of businesses and disciplines. GCI (the investment bank) has grown in a quantum fashion over the last few years. It is virtually impossible to meet all of the counterparts within the investment bank let alone across the entire organization. We really had very little contact to the other divisions so it was becoming very difficult to understand business needs or see any commonality in our businesses."

Maffucci continues, "We were finding that the traditional strategy of individual development of current and future executives was not working. Executives from one part of the organization did not feel compelled to work with their colleagues in another part because they believed that their business strategy and objectives were so different from their colleagues'."

Hence, a change in strategy for management development became a pressing concern. As Rolf E. Breuer explains, "The reason I decided to commission the program was that I have so many detail problems on my desk that I can't see the forest through the trees. And the reason I have a large part of these problems is that Mr. X in New York isn't collaborating with—or even talking to—Mr. Y in Frankfurt, and Mr. Jones from business area A in London is not working with Ms. Smith from business area B in Singapore. If we are to achieve anything we must first learn to communicate and work as a team."

Therefore, Deutsche Bank began exploring the development of a customized approach to executive education that would supplement the usage of the existing open-enrollment programs. The vision of Breuer was that the new approach to management learning would combine the classical executive education programs available at leading business schools with elements of organizational and personal development needed for success at Deutsche Bank.

To realize this new in-house executive education practice, Deutsche Bank searched for an external learning partner from the world of leading business schools. The search criteria Deutsche Bank used to locate an optimal university partner included three major areas: brand of school, structural capabilities of the school and the cultural fit between Deutsche Bank and the school. These criteria specifically are shown in Figure 3-2.

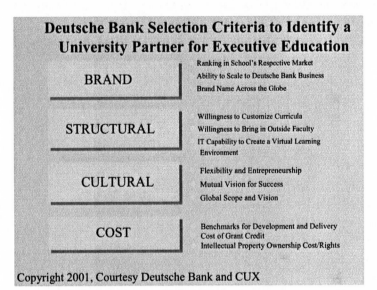

Figure 3-2

CEO Breuer says, "We chose Duke University, Fuqua School of Business, for their ability to provide a learning environment for faculty and Deutsche Bank executives to work in learning groups both at the Fuqua School of Business (FSB) campus and via the FSB virtual learning environment. The virtual learning environment helps participants and faculty to exchange views, continue to work together, discuss the state of the projects, and gauge the progress being made."

As the strongest supporter for the new learning model Breuer naturally chose to be the sponsor of the first program. With his strong support, a new approach to executive education was successfully developed using many of the elements of the new learning model—just-in-time learning, self-managed learning and a distributed learning environment—which, when taken together more strongly combine learning and work.

The first executive education program in this series was called the Spokesman's Challenge in honor of the sponsorship of CEO Breuer. Participants in the program include twenty senior managers from various business divisions and many geographical regions. The opening meeting brought these twenty managers together with Breuer to discuss the rationale for the program and the results expected at completion. Figure 3-3 illustrates how learning is used at Deutsche Bank to accelerate change.

Breuer describes this new approach to learning as significantly different from a course in which you go off to a conference center for two weeks and are told by business school faculty what other firms have done and why. Rather, it requires individuals to use "real time" business challenges to solve organizational issues.

CEO Breuer identified four challenges as:

1. What are the cultural and organizational characteristics of a truly global firm? What would Deutsche Bank need to improve in order to be one?

2. What are the characteristics of successful matrix organizations? What should the bank do in order to get maximum benefit from its own matrix organization?

3. What needs to change for Deutsche Bank to become more innovative and entrepreneurial? How do these changes occur?

4. How can Deutsche Bank better manage knowledge as a critical resource for business success?

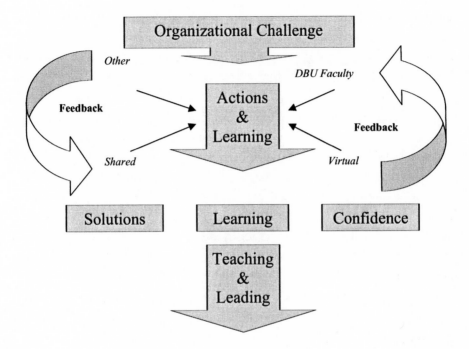

Figure 3-3: Learning as a Motor for Change

c. 2001, courtesy of Deutsche Bank

It is important to note that the commissioning of Spokesman's Challenge was not simply the beginning of a new era in executive education at Deutsche Bank—but the result of a period of major change for the organization. In fact, much of the impetus for the implementation of the new learning model was driven by the new organization at Deutsche Bank—five business divisions and a streamlined Corporate Center. The resulting Spokesman's Challenge required participants across the five business divisions and corporate to work and learn together.

Breuer says, "Spokesman's Challenge was our trial attempt to work in cooperation with the faculty of a leading business school to create a learning program that builds on prior work in the bank. Spokesman's Challenge is also a different way of learning, of exchanging views and ideas, and applying this knowledge to help Deutsche Bank achieve our mission of becoming the world's best financial services provider."

Spokesman's Challenge: Design for Success

One of the key success factors for Spokesman's Challenge success was Breuer himself and his personal involvement throughout each stage of the program's development.

The development of an executive education program such as Spokesman's Challenge follows three stages. The following outlines the three stages of the Spokesman's Challenge, as well as the issues that impact the successful conclusion of such a program:

Stage 1: Contracting and identification of a problem. The first stage is initiated through the identification of problems—such as increasing market share or creating a common vision—that require a detailed examination. These challenges create the foundation for a new approach to learning at Deutsche Bank.

Stage 2: The program, action, and learning. Although the programs vary in style, they all have three strands of action in common: personal development, the management of a complex project, and the testing of relevant theories and models. In addition, they also have in common full sessions of the entire group of participants, action-learning team events, and working and learning in a virtual environment.

The participants are tutored by faculty and subject matter experts from the Duke University network as well as by relevant experts from within the bank. They are each provided with the technology to allow them to handle the virtual learning platform. Each project has an active sponsor to whom the participants, divided into teams, report on progress and from whom they receive indications and support. An important aspect of all the programs is when the teams prepare a presentation and a report outlining their recommendations.

Reports one participant, "The faculty and facilitators worked as a bridge to all the members of our globally distributed team. They kept the dialog going and reengaged individuals who had fallen out of the discussion. In addition they provided us with a theoretical framework based on external references, best practices, and leading business thinking for our research. When it came time to present our initial ideas to Dr. Breuer, they helped us keep our focus on what was important and what was actionable so that we didn't offer unrealizable recommendations."

During the virtual work on their topics, the participants are expected to manage their own learning by accessing the resources within the bank and the university as well as in other organizations, libraries, and the Internet. They are also expected not to jump to premature and simple solutions but instead to encourage each other to see familiar things in a different light. The tutors from the bank or the Duke network support this process of critical reflection in the early stages of the project development. An important element of this reflection is the participant's personal contribution as an executive staff member, a team member, and an individual.

An executive education faculty advisor from Duke's Fuqua School of Business describes the participants as "normally very busy and very results oriented so they can jump to the first solution that appears acceptable in the name of time efficiency. It is my role to make sure the team is not simply addressing the symptoms of the problem but really pushing the envelope."

During the entire program, the participants are expected to remain in contact with each other and with the sponsor. These regular reports on the progress of the project serve the sponsor as an important feedback loop and ensure that the project remain on course. It also involves the sponsors, who are mostly from top management in the learning process.

Each team submits a project proposal to the sponsor. This report is no different from that submitted by a consultant and contains all the elements from the presentation to the interpretation of the problem to plans of action including estimates of costs and resources. This feedback process opens up a new level of learning to the participants, namely that of the development of a disciplined approach to problem solving, of presentation and influencing, and also of political skills, all of which are very important for future executives. A contact is established between senior and top management, which would otherwise not arise, or at least not with such a depth of content.

Stage 3: Handling the results. The extent to which the proposed recommendations and plans of action are implemented depends on their quality, the determination of the sponsor, and the sensitive transfer of the responsibility for implementation to a department or another project group.

"I found the recommendations of the Spokesman's Challenge teams so encouraging," Breuer says, "that I asked four of my colleagues on the Executive Board to each sponsor one of the learning teams and to pursue their recommendations and identify ways to implement them in the bank."

Results generated from these programs are shared with colleagues at the bank and deposited in the virtual library as the core of Deutsche Bank University. These projects provide insight for other groups as they pursue their projects.

As one executive education participant points out, "The work done by the previous groups has been quite helpful to our group. Although our projects are very different from last year's projects, there are a couple of major themes that run through all of them. It has been quite interesting, and a big help to us, to see how last year's teams looked at some of these themes. Their discussions have served as a starting point for some of our discussions and having access to their research has saved us from duplicating their work."

The alumni from these programs are expected to change from learners to teachers as they communicate what they have learned. Typical is this participant's comment: "The manor of dialogue and idiom that was developed during the course of our teamwork in Spokesman's Challenge has proven quite useful outside the program's environment. I now engage my staff in the same sort of dialogue to solve problems, challenge assumptions, or get to the source of disagreement. I believe we, my staff and I, have improved our overall performance by increasing our ability to overcome the hurdles which stand between us and our objectives."

A number of graduates have become peer advisors or mentors for other executive education programs. An executive education peer advisor says, "I'm really looking forward to being a peer advisor to this year's Spokesman's Challenge groups. I hope that this year's participants will use me as a sounding board to test their ideas and solutions. I also believe we can help this year's participants avoid some of the difficulties and dead ends we had to deal with and avoid duplicating work that has already been done."

One of the most desirable results of the design of these programs is an increased confidence in one's own ability to understand sophisticated strategic issues and solve complex problems successfully; this applies to individuals as well as the entire organization. Initial feedback from former participants indicates that this increased confidence has led to a feeling that they are empowered to engage successfully in activities of strategic significance to the bank.

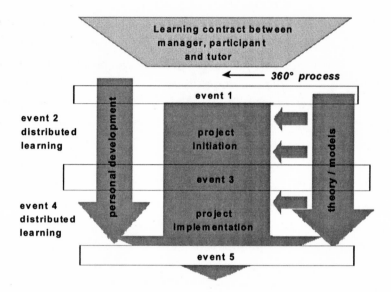

Figure 3-4: Standard structure of the Spokesman's Challenge

Spokesman's Challenge Structure

The standard structure of the Spokesman's Challenge is outlined in Figure 3-4. A program can have three, five, or more events and combines personal development, project work, teaching, and distribution of theoretical frameworks and models related to the projects. These lead to four different kinds of learning:

- Learning for the individual participants
- Development of a shared mindset and a corps spirit within the class
- Recommendations and findings for organizational problems to be presented to the sponsor.
- Participants as learner-teachers.

There was a very real pioneer feeling among the participants, faculty, and Deutsche Bank program managers as Breuer initiated the Spokesman's Challenge. He continued to build on the open environment for change that had been generated from the Spokesman's Challenge.

One of the most important outcomes of the Spokesman's Challenge is the creation of a mission statement and a set of core values that are currently being deployed throughout Deutsche Bank. "It's comparatively easy to come up with the values, its more difficult to implement them," one participant came to realize. "The challenge now is to reinforce these values and this has to come from the top down—every single member of senior management, including the members of the Executive Board, have to live these values day by day."

Tennessee Valley Authority: "Pathways to Excellence"

The largest wholesale generator of electric power in the United States, the Tennessee Valley Authority has made great strides in the last several years to unify education and training for its 13,000 employees. TVA University, created in 1994, was charged with consolidating all training, eliminating redundant programs and aligning training with strategic plans.

"Our primary reason for starting TVA University was to address a practical need," says former TVA chairman Craven Crowell. "In 1993, we were using education and training only as a tactical solution, with education and training confined within each organizational silo. It was a fragmented, redundant, and expensive system.

"To improve quality, consistency, and efficiency, we consolidated these units under Tennessee Valley Authority University (TVAU), making it the central portal for all learning and development. This lowered our costs and linked our education and training to business goals," added Crowell.

Crowell was instrumental in encouraging TVAU to not only develop internal learning programs but also to offer portable credentials for TVA employees.

"We never intended to meet every education and training need internally," says Mary Catherine Hammer, 6 TVAU General Manager. "It has always been our position to form partnerships with local colleges and universities. We identified institutions that had the flexibility and the desire to work within our corporate needs. For example, our requirements included the use of distance learning as an instructional tool and offering classes after hours or on weekends."

Because business concepts and strategies continue to evolve, TVA also wanted a comprehensive menu of courses available as TVA's managers developed work-related needs. In short, the TVA University team headed by Hammer searched for an academic partner to provide a flexible, comprehensive, just-in-time executive learning program.

So, in 1996, TVA University piloted an EMBA program through the business college of the University of Tennessee at Chattanooga (UTC). UTC's College of Business possessed a fully accredited and comprehensive EMBA program with a strong international learning component.

University Partnerships: Continuing Education Units

In addition to the degree-based programs, TVA University has also partnered with Tennessee Technological University to validate TVA learning materials and award continuing education units (CEUs) to participants in such areas as human resources, clerical and engineering.

"Employees can't take their skills for granted," says Crowell. "In the computer industry, state-of-the-art machines quickly become obsolete. It's the same with jobs. A good job today might be gone tomorrow, and unless employees have learned other skills that are valued and needed by the company, they will be gone, too. No employee can afford to fall asleep with regard to his or her skill level, education, or their employment," he says.

United Technologies Corporation: Birth of the Employee Scholar Program

George David, chairman and CEO of United Technologies, a manufacturer of products ranging from jet engines to elevators, is a business leader whose life and work are about continuous education. He is known for an insatiable curiosity, and he encourages this trait among employees. He has spoken out often about the importance of corporate education—and has backed up these statements with considerable corporate resources. He also has committed UTC resources to the improvement of the struggling school system in UTC's headquarters city, Hartford, Connecticut. And he has made a personal $10 million contribution to his alma mater, the Darden School of Business at the University of Virginia.

As with fellow CEOs, David's public statements respond to social as well as business issues of the day, but there is one theme he returns to time and again in his speeches: continuous lifelong education.

David typically waits for all points of view to be heard and sometimes repeated, and often invoking the "24-hour rule," an overnight cooling-off period that ensures intellect rather than emotion in decision making. But he was more eager than usual to implement an idea he introduced in late 1995: prepaid tuition and education fees for all employees; paid time off to study; no limitation on subject matter and; upon graduation, an award of company stock.

"Too expensive," said some managers about the stock award. "Too hard to administer," said others. "There'll be chaos on the factory floor," said still others. And "people will get their degrees on our nickel and leave," most said.

But David rebuffed these pleas. The new program was the right thing to do for the company and its employees.

He communicated his point of view succinctly when he announced the program before a group of journalists, legislators, and employees at the National Press Club. He said, "As a private employer, we cannot guarantee anyone a job, but we are nonetheless obliged to provide employees reasonable opportunities to reestablish themselves, ideally on more favorable conditions, in the event of job loss."

Today, more than 12,000 UTC employees are embracing their futures through the company's Employee Scholar Program (ESP), more than double the number of just four years ago. They are hourly workers and salaried professionals. They include high-potential managers and engineers working at the forefront of technology. A growing number of employee scholars can be found at company locations in Hangzhou, China; São Bernardo do Campo, Brazil; St. Petersburg, Russia; and elsewhere in the global UTC organization.

ESP had its beginning when George David discovered that only four percent of UTC U.S. employees were receiving tuition reimbursement. He couldn't understand why 96 percent of our employees were passing up this opportunity. The company was willing to provide employees with a free education, and yet most were walking away from this exceptional benefit."

The reasons were varied. Actually, each of UTC's business units had its own educational assistance program. Reimbursements ranged from 50 to 100 percent of the cost of tuition. Students had to pay up front and were reimbursed upon successfully completing a course. Fees and books were not always covered. Employees were not given time off for study. And they had to enroll in programs that related to their jobs, subject to their supervisors' approval.

After the ESP took effect on January 1, 1996, for all U.S. employees, UTC extended the program the following year to the 183 countries in which the company does business.

In mid-1999, UTC extended the program even further—to employees who had lost their jobs through downsizing. The company announced that employees being laid off could remain in the ESP for a year. UTC said the purpose was to enable employees to earn a degree that would help improve their job prospects in the future.

Approximately 12,000 employees have participated worldwide in ESP since inception, including more than 10,000 in the United States and some 2,000 abroad. Nearly 1,600 U.S. employees and 83 international employees earned degrees in 1999 (through September). In the United

States and abroad, about three of every four participants are salaried employees and the rest are hourly.

Participation has grown dramatically outside of the United States. The number of non-U.S. employees participating doubled from 1997 to 1998, reaching a modest two percent of the international work force, and the company expected to report another large increase for 1999 when year-end numbers were tallied. The greatest numbers of employee-students outside the United States have been in Mexico, Brazil, Canada, and the Philippines.

But the ESP is just one part of United Technologies' comprehensive approach to employee education. Thousands of other UTC employees are taking hundreds of non-degree courses in employee development, quality improvement, supply management, and many other subjects. This education extends all the way to top executives, who take programs that cut across all UTC businesses.

Many companies offer tuition reimbursement plans, but United Technologies believes its program is unique in terms of the broad combination of benefits. UTC may be the only company to provide reimbursement without limitations while also giving time off for study *and* awarding stock as a reward for earning a degree.

How does UTC Employee Scholar Program compare to educational programs offered by other companies?

Hewitt Associates LLC, an educational consulting firm in Lincolnshire, Illinois, released a report in June 1999 on corporate educational reimbursement plans. The report summarized a survey of 460 medium and large employers conducted in 1998. Among the major survey findings:

• Most educational reimbursement plans (86 percent) impose one or more types of limits on the amount reimbursed for tuition and expenses. UTC has no limits.

- Two-thirds of employers (67 percent) set a minimum service requirement, with six months and one year the most common service requirements. UTC employees are eligible from day one of employment.

- Most employers (76 percent) reimburse only after successful completion of a course. Only 5 percent always pay before the course
  begins. UTC pays tuition and expenses to the institution up front,
  at registration.

- Most companies require that courses relate to the employer's business. Only 8 percent of employers reimburse for non-business
  courses unrelated to the employer's business or not required as part
  of a degree program. UTC employees are reimbursed for any courses
  they take, whether or not they are job-related, although employees
  have some tax liability when courses do not relate to the employee's
  work.

NCR Corporation:
Learning Partnerships with the Business Units

At NCR Corporation, the data systems manufacturer, CEO sponsorship and support is evident in several division-wide activities and senior
management learning initiatives. These are activities that integrate a business function and learning. "We're finding one thing that works for us is
to integrate learning into other things that are going on in the organization," says Bradley Luckhaupt, NCR's vice president for global learning.
In one example, the senior executive who manages NCR's financial business, which manufacturers automated teller machines, decided in 1999
that he wanted to have written training development plans for each of the
division's top 200 managers.

These personalized plans would be managed in cooperation with their
supervisors. NCR Global Learning came up with a personalized curriculum map (a set of courses built around a job) for each manager. Each
individual's map would spell out the required skills, and the recom-

mended training to build those competencies. The objective in this skills mapping exercise was to increase the retention rate of management-level employees, and simultaneously build up the skills of division managers worldwide.

To announce the program, NCR Global Learning partnered with NCR human resources to webcast the new program's features and benefits; including how to create a curriculum map using NCR's online university.

Using the system's real-time curriculum mapping, a sales person in the ATM business would go into NCR's online university, look for their job description (say, sales manager). The system would then list all the competencies critical to the success of their job. It would also ask some questions about what they do, such as regions of the world where they work, and the type of equipment they sell. The online curriculum mapping tool would then go on to build a curriculum map designed to address the competencies for that job.

The outcome of this curriculum mapping process is to list all possible development opportunities such as classroom courses, web-based online courses, written materials or CD-ROM learning. A participating manager can do an online registration for any course, and also order online any course materials such as books or manuals. Luckhaupt says that other NCR divisions have expressed interest in building their own curriculum mapping programs, with the assistance of NCR Global Learning.

Learning initiatives such as this one have the support of NCR's senior management, including CEO Lars Nyberg. In designing training programs, NCR Global Learning has a partnership with each business unit or NCR division. As Luckhaupt says: "We partner with them in learning solutions. And they prioritize them, not us. The business leaders have to be involved in prioritization and sponsorship. So if we don't have those relationships with the senior managers in each of the divisions we're dead."

Luckhardt continues, "We've changed over the last five years to go from I call 'bottoms up' personal self-driven development to now more strategically driven 'tops down' initiatives. What caused that? Top down is linked more to the company's results. If you want to be more linked to the strategy, you've got to create learning opportunities that are top down in order to win the respect of the business managers. If you don't have solid relationships with the business units, you can easily become disconnected. Then you're just offering courses to help people improve themselves rather than achieve business directives."

Chapter Summary

Chief executives have becoming active supporters of a range of learning programs, including company-wide e-learning, management development programs, and academic partnerships that support organizational goals.

The corporate university functions as a facilitator in designing these learning programs, often in cooperation with business unit managers, and in all situations, with the active support of the CEO and senior management team. In some organizations, the CEO has become "The Education CEO," championing new education initiatives such as George David's (CEO UTC) Employee Scholar Program or Michael Dell's "I Know the Net." The distinguishing feature is active involvement of the CEO in creating the vision for how to align learning to business goals and then holding his team accountable for these objectives.

Action Steps:
Getting The CEO To Sponsor Education
and Lifelong Learning

1) Find out what the CEO must accomplish in the organization and then propose how learning will align with these goals.

2) Set up an advisory group of business line managers to help shape the curriculum development process and ensure curriculum maps meet their business challenges.

3) Set up individual meetings with each business manager. Rather than sell the recommendation top down be sure to include at least one of their suggestions into your overall design and their contributions to the final product will build enthusiasm for the project.

4) Maintain an on-going dialogue with this group of business managers. Ask for their output continuously. Include them as senior advisors in keeping the program targeted and linked to business goals.

5) Obtain business manager guidance to create a metrics system so learning is measured according to specific goals.

Lesson #3

**Develop an Advisory Board to support,
direct and review your company's education function**

▼

CHAPTER FOUR:

THE CEO AS GOVERNOR

"A governor oversees the machinery of laws and resources that benefit the commonwealth, the common good. An effective governor makes sure that that machinery is running smoothly. My role in governing learning at Bain is to make sure that our machinery is functioning efficiently and effectively, that we're working on the right things in the best way, and that the right people—the best human assets—are working together."

—*Tom Tierney, Bain & Company*

As governor of corporate learning, the chief executive officer takes an active role in managing the learning and developing programs of the organization. These functions may include any of the following roles: reviewing goals and objectives, providing direction on measuring the effectiveness of learning, and evaluating outcomes. In this capacity, the CEO may be an active, "hands on," manager. Some CEOs govern by meeting regularly with the chief learning officer and reviewing (and approving) learning programs.

A governance structure provides the administrative support necessary to bring to life the learning vision of senior management and put words into action. Management support for restructuring the corporate education function is often the catalyst for creating a corporate university or enterprise-wide learning function. It begins with a management directive to align training activities with the organization's goals and objectives. The long-term management objective might be recruiting and retaining the best qualified employees in a tight labor market. It might be enhancing shareholder value, and the intrinsic value of the corporation or fending off a hostile takeover.

While, strong support from the top is critically important in getting an enterprise-wide learning function off the ground, a formal governance structure is also an essential element. A coalition of business unit managers, each having designated responsibilities, is necessary to give the effort a critical mass in the early stages of growth. This governance group should include some, though not all, of the top managers of the organization. Some managers aren't willing to contribute their time; others say they won't get involved in a "risky" venture. A good team leader will learn to work with senior managers who decide to participate in learning activities, and consult with those who choose not to become actively involved.

Research by Corporate University Xchange shows that many corporate CEOs get regular updates on learning/training issues by their Chief Learning Officer. While more than 50% of CLOs still report to the head of Human Resources, a growing number are now reporting directly to the CEO (see Figure 4-1). This bolsters the view that CLOs enjoy growing recognition in the organization, and that many CLOs are regarded as equivalent to the Chief Information Officer or Chief Financial Officer.

Corporate Universities Reporting to Human Resources or CEO/President, by Industry

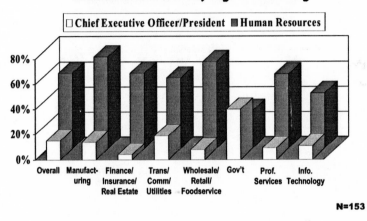

Figure 4-1

c2001 Corporate University Xchange

Sometimes, the chief executive officer gets personally involved in organizing a governance council. Michael Dell, CEO of Dell Computer, created the Dell Learning Board of Regents, an advisory panel responsible for setting policy, directing and reviewing all learning activities within Dell. Board members include the vice presidents of three major operating groups, along with the vice presidents of finance and human resources. The president of Dell Learning is a non-voting member and secretary to the board. The Dell Learning Board of Regents has a charter that includes:

- Review and approve company-wide budget and conformity to budget
- Establish standards, budgets and strategic direction for Dell Learning

- Review and approve resources for annual regional education plans
- Review measurement of training effectiveness
- Review utilization of facilities
- Review information technology requirements of learning
- Review new education priorities and build versus buy proposals
- Review course maintenance proposals
- Understand delivery strategies and set goals for the upcoming year
- Hear presentations by Dell Learning staff on new learning/training initiatives

The Dell Learning Board of Regents charter shows the range of decision-making powers of the governing board. Research conducted by Corporate University Xchange supports the functions of the Dell Learning Board of Regents . Figure 4-2 is based upon interviews with 175 Chief Learning Officers on the typical functions of a governing board., uncovered five functions of a governing board.

Figure 4-2: The Five Functions of a Corporate Governance Structure

1. *Identifying and prioritizing current and future learning needs.* What are the company's learning needs in relation to business strategies? What new skills do employees need to perform their jobs effectively?

2. *Linking training to these key business strategies.* What are the investment priorities of the business? How should learning/training be linked to business strategies?

3. *Ensuring consistent design, development, delivery and measurement.* What are the procedures, processes and standards to determine if training is the best solution? How should learning programs be designed and delivered?

4. *Providing direction for the development of a philosophy for learning.* What is the organization's learning philosophy? Will the organization

develop a culture of continuous learning? How will this learning philosophy be communicated throughout the organization.

5. *Review outcomes in investment in learning.* Evaluate benchmark investment against actual investment. Probe outcomes in terms of increased employee retention, productivity, achievement of sales goals.

C 2001, Corporate University Xchange

Bain & Company's Managing Director Plays Multiple Governing Roles

Thomas Tierney, former worldwide managing director at Bain & Company, performs his role as governor of learning at Bain in three ways: as overseer, organizational designer, and asset builder.

Overseer. Assesses how successful the company is in meeting its learning goals. Tierney points to a worldwide training audit as one of his pivotal evaluation initiatives as overseer. This audit strongly influenced Tierney to overhaul Bain's training organization.

Prior to 1997, management of learning at Bain was the responsibility of an administrative-staff training director, who reported to a primarily client-dedicated Bain vice president. In addition to managing the training function, the training director also oversaw other administrative areas, such as case-team support, the corporate library, and an experience-sharing database network. "In essence," Tierney notes, "training was a part-time initiative. We had a client partner with a 10 percent training allocation managing a staff person with a 25 percent training allocation. Even at the time we knew it wasn't the best way to manage. But considering our situation leading up to and flowing from our reorganization in the late 80s, it served us well, up to a point."

To reduce overhead and still provide basic training, Bain decentralized its training programs. "Those that were managed from the center—both in terms of content and logistics—were farmed out to many of our other offices," Tierney explains. "London took over worldwide Manager

Training and Experienced Consultant Training for our European offices. San Francisco assumed responsibility for North America Experienced Consultant Training. Our Paris office got New Consultant Training, and Boston retained the flagship Associate Consultant Training program." The result, Tierney suggests, had many positive aspects. "Program content and learning approaches were reworked under fresh leadership. We got more people involved in learning across our network. Ownership of programs really blossomed once we relocated a lot of program management from the corporate center to our local offices. And we groomed a new generation of teacher-learners in the process."

Over time, however, the gains from decentralization were offset by emerging weaknesses, particularly in the ways locally managed training programs interacted to create a coordinated and comprehensive approach to career development. Training efforts under local management were allowed to go their own way; inevitably, these programs became increasingly disconnected from Bain's senior management and lacked a unifying theme or vision. "After a few years," Tierney notes, "it became apparent that we had to create central management of education, while retaining the benefits of decentralized ownership, input, and participation."

To overcome decentralization-related deficiencies in the training organization, the audit recommended that the firm appoint a worldwide training director with 100 percent allocation to overseeing the Bain learning function. It also reorganized the corporate training department in Boston to beef up coordination of program content and logistical support while retaining local sponsorship for many programs. Consequently, many regional programs, such as Experienced Consultant Training, were merged as worldwide offerings to better utilize faculty and other training resources. In each office, coordinators were appointed to oversee office training and locally administered corporate programs, and to improve communication with the corporate training center.

Organizational designer. Ensures that the values, structures, and people are in place at Bain to sustain a learning system that relies on networking rather than hierarchy: "I preside over dynamic and fluid structures. And these structures should distill into a highly concentrated, flatter organization geared totally to exponential learning. It's the only way it's going to happen."

As far as participating in designing systems for learning, Tierney evokes the "clock-builder" image popularized in James C. Collins and Jerry I. Porras' best-selling book, *Built to Last: Successful Habits of Visionary Companies*. According to Tierney, a clock builder facilitates the interpersonal connections that generate learning, "making it easy for the right people to talk to each other at the right time."

But his focus on systems and structures does not mean that Tierney sees learning design as a dry process. He hopes that as organizational designer, he can "create an environment in which people can touch their own passion for learning."

Asset builder. Places managing the human assets as a critical responsibility. Tierney focuses on developing others' ability to add value through one-on-one contact (*e.g.,* teaching and mentoring), modeling behavior, and influencing structures—and influencing behaviors within those structures—to maximize learning and client results. He spends a great deal of his time out of his Boston headquarters traveling to other offices and programs, listening to his colleagues around the network, and speaking out about the firm's values as well as lifetime Bain relationships as employees and alumni.

Moreover, to generate optimum return on Bain's investment in its human resources, Tierney works hard to target "learning zealots" and to elevate them to key leadership positions. Tierney also sees the need to discard practices aimed at "maintaining our intellectual purity." Breaking out of the intellectual purity mindset has meant instituting nontraditional management policies. For example, in order to refresh learning throughout the Bain network, Tierney will rotate an office director from time to time, not as a disciplinary measure, but in the interests of keeping learning fresh and vital for both the individual and the team. According to this practice, the former office head usually returns to full-time client work. At Bain, rotating an office director is not seen as a demotion, but rather as a way of multiplying opportunities for learning. "Job rotation at this level," Tierney states, "keeps the office heads from getting stale. This way we can capitalize on the expertise of a seasoned officer and introduce into the position fresh, unpredictable insights."

Tierney recognizes that looking beyond traditional business-school recruiting is another way of overcoming the constraints of Bain's intellectual purity. At Bain, this means aggressively increasing the number of new hires wooed from relevant industries. For Tierney, "learning is the number one value we gain from industry hires."

Another of Tierney's asset-building challenges emerges from the graying of the firm's leadership. "How do we capture and perpetuate the wisdom learned from our first-generation leaders?" he asks. One solution Tierney is working on involves the creation of Bain "fellows" and director *emeritus* appointments to enhance mentoring and firm oversight.

Asset building extends beyond the current roster of Bain employees. The firm's alumni program has contributed significantly to Tierney's attempts to expand the company's learning network. "We want to see Bain as a lifetime relationship that may span several careers," Tierney suggests. "Our alumni are 'from us,' but no longer 'of us,' you might say. They know us, how we think, what we value. But they also can infuse our thinking with the richness of non-Bain experience. Obviously, with all these Bain alumni out there, we want—we can't afford *not* to maintain positive and productive alumni relations. This also works positively against any inclination to maintain our intellectual purity."

Tierney also sees case-team staffing as an opportunity to build Bain's human assets. He maintains that promoting broad membership in practice areas helps overcome case-team myopia. "In principle," he says, "you don't want 'dedicated' thinkers because dedicated thinkers create fire walls against spreading ideas. That doesn't mean we don't nurture experts. But it does mean that we're trying to create a learning architecture where Bain people learn in a variety of contexts."

Reviewing the potential scope and complexity of the audit, Tierney readily saw the need to involve high-level leadership throughout the Bain system to ensure quality decision-making, buy-in, and implementation. His first step was to create the Worldwide Training Advisory Group, composed of Steven Tallman, Bain's former vice president of training, and five senior partners: one partner each from North America, Asia, and Europe; the head of Bain's Strategy Practice; and the partner for VP Professional Development. First convened in 1997, this committee meets quarterly to influence the firm's training strategy and to monitor implementation of training initiatives. The group also presents Tierney with an annual report on training-strategy-related milestones and issues.

Corporate University Annual Reports

Corporate University Xchange has uncovered the concept of creating an Annual Report summarizing the training and learning results, increasingly critical to the ongoing management of the learning function. Just as a CEO highlights a company's accomplishments, the dean of a corporate learning function must also create a communication tool. Table 4-3 shows the Table of Contents from the 1999 First University (First Union Corporation) Annual Report.

Figure 4-3: Corporate University and Annual Reports:
What Are They Reporting?
Table of Contents—First University Annual Report

Our Organization
  Mission & Purpose
  History of First University
  HR Board of Trustees & Role
  First University's 1999 Strategic Focus
  First University Infrastructure
  First University Organizational Chart

First University At-A-Glance
  "Quick Hit" Highlights
  1999 Results Indicators for First University

University Highlights
>Professional Accomplishments
>1998 Business Leadership Award Winners
>In-Depth Highlights
>Ready Talent
>Discover First Union
>Leadership Discovery Overview
>1999 HR Essential Broadcasts
>Room Reservation System (EMS)
>Telephone Registration System (CARY)

College/Team Highlights
>Automation & Operations College
>>Results Indicators
>Consumer College
>>Results Indicators
>E-Commerce/Specialty Finance College
>>Results Indicators
>First University Services
>Human Resources College
>New Leadership College
>>Results Indicators
>Wholesale Banking College
>Commercial College
>Investment College
>Capital Market College
>Results Indicators

Reference
>First University Contact Information
>First University Locations
>First University Acronyms

Dell Computer's Founder is an Active Governor

It may seem obvious that the CEO would be the ultimate decision-maker regarding any aspect of the company, yet in many organizations the executive staff, and certainly the office of the CEO, remains uninvolved in training decisions. Not so at Dell, where the company's founder put himself on the interview team when it came time to hire the head of Dell Learning. Recalling the interview, John Coné, President of Dell Learning says, "I have to admit that the first time I met with Michael, I had to get over how young he was. He's pretty used to that, and I think he cut me a little slack. I had been warned that he was very interested in training, but I still wondered if this was going to be one of those obligatory meetings with the top guy. That curiosity lasted only a few seconds. I was impressed with how engaged he was on the subject. He spent at least as much time asking me what he could do as he did asking what I expected to bring to the function. A big part of my decision to join Dell was knowing that I had an ally in the CEO who was willing to be hands-on."

As the function took shape, Dell's new VP of Learning took a page from his previous experience at Motorola, forming governing councils populated by senior executives from the key businesses and functions throughout Dell. The chairs of those councils, all company vice presidents, made policy and set direction in areas like management, sales, and quality education. The decisions of each of the councils had to be ratified by the Board of Regents of Dell Learning.

The mission of the Dell Board of Regents is to set policy, support, direct, and review the operation of education within Dell.

Dell Learning: Why a Board of Regents

Education is a primary lever for shaping the culture of Dell. It delivers key messages about the expectations of management and employees. It is also a competitive weapon. The Dell educational efforts are aimed at producing a workforce that can surpass the competition and exceed customer expectations.

Management, especially senior management, must be the champions of education for the company. Training must be directly linked to strategic business issues that are determined from the leadership of the company. Furthermore, those needs must be prioritized and appropriate funding approved by the leadership.

A typical agenda for the board meeting at Dell Learning is illustrated in Figure 4-4.

Figure 4-4: Agenda Items for Dell Learning Board of Regents

1. Review last year's results.
   a. Training delivered
   b. Income and expense
   c. Training developed
   d. Budget conformance
   e. Utilization of staff and facilities
   f. Training effectiveness data
   g. Special problems or issues dealt with
   h. Results compared to any other objectives that were set
   i. Establish (or review) standards, budgets, and strategic direction for
Dell Learning.
2. Review proposed education priorities.
   a. Functional roadmaps as proposed by councils
   b. Priorities indicated in regional education plans
   c. Executive development priorities
   d. IT systems requirements
3. Review recommended policies or policy changes.

4. Review and approve major decisions requiring board action, e.g., cross functional training program where attendance will be critical and the development costs will be significant.

5. Review training and acquisition budget.

6. Presentations on projects or programs by the training staff for information and education of the board (at their request).

C 2001 courtesy of Dell Computer Corporation

Functional Advisory Councils at Dell Learning

Although Dell is a regionalized company, Dell Learning established Functional Advisory Councils in the areas of Quality, Management, Technology, and Sales/Marketing.

The mission of these Functional Advisory Councils is to guarantee that the educational priorities of each function are identified and met. The roles of the Functional Advisory Councils are:

- Approve an overall education roadmap for the function
- Identify unmet training needs
- Determine priorities for new programs to be acquired or developed
- Review the impact (ROI) of education on the function and establish priorities for formal follow-up evaluation on specific courses.
- Review and approving recommendations to discontinue courses
- Identify Subject Matter Experts for roles on training development teams and project committees, or as instructors

The Functional Advisory Councils are made up of vice president-level managers worldwide. They were selected based on their interest in the area of focus as well as their responsibility for the functional area involved. In a few cases, director level members were selected to insure representation of key regions or technical areas. In essence, the advisory councils developed recommendations in their areas of focus that were then forwarded to the Board of Regents for final approval.

Functional Advisory Councils come and go at Dell, depending on current needs. As time passed, and making decisions concerning training became a natural part of management activities, the topical councils were replaced by councils within the businesses. The move was a pretty logical one, since the members of the various advisory boards were, essentially, the top management team for the business or the function. The old-style advisory councils are still convened on an ad hoc basis, but the real work of governance is now done in the same way as any other strategic aspect of management. Today, the items once handled by the Board of Regents, which had always consisted of members of Dell's Executive Committee, have become a part of the regular Executive Committee agenda. Functions like Finance and Information Technology still convene training councils, and company-wide councils for Marketing and Engineering still meet as well.

This active involvement is now so natural at Dell that it is virtually invisible. But it represents a critical shift from common practice. For example, in many of the specialized functional areas, like training, executives can't be expected to know what they can delegate and what they need to manage more closely.

A key at Dell is involving the CEO (and other execs) at the right level. Dell Learning doesn't ask Michael Dell to review course designs or curriculum plans, but rather to approve strategies and evaluate the bottom line impact they produce. Here are some examples of decisions made by the Dell Learning Board of Regents in the corporate university's first year of existence:

Typical Governance Issues at Dell Learning

- As a guideline, all employees at Dell should receive a minimum of 40 hours of training each year. (This guideline was later dropped in favor of one that said each person should have a training plan and get the training spelled out in that plan.)

- All managers should be required to have Education Plans for their organizations that reflect appropriate levels of education based on the requirements of their business, the competencies required for the various roles in that business, and the gaps between current and desired performance.

- Dell Learning corporate should move to Tuition-Based Education in order to put control of key decisions on training into the hands of the users.

- Dell Learning corporate should move to a minimum of 40 percent Non-Classroom Training. (The current goal is 70 percent and moving upward.)

- Educational investments should be held at current levels. (Dell tracks training investments as a percent of payroll.) We should benchmark levels of investment at selected companies in order to make informed investment decisions.

Education Reviews at Dell Computer

Another example of CEO involvement in governance at Dell Computer is found in how the work of the education function is measured. Dell's training organization has historically had it's own operations review with the Office of the Chair (OOC). Those quarterly sessions review the total company investment in learning, the areas of focus, the deployment of resources around the company, and the results being achieved. In addition, the OOC looks at training department productivity comparisons of Dell's investments to other world-class companies (those benchmarks that the Board of Regents insisted on in the first year). A copy of all the benchmarks and the Dell Learning Annual Report can be found at **http://www.dell.com/us/en/gen/corporate/dellu_ar_99_ER.htm**.

But there's another, more subtle way in which Dell's CEO is involved in setting strategic direction for training—by personally identifying some of the targets for that training. Michael Dell's two vice chairs directed a study to identify the core competencies needed for leadership success at Dell. The study determined which competencies the company should require of the people they hire, which can be developed, and which are most likely to cause an executive to fail. These competencies have been integrated into Dell's staffing, promotion, and performance review processes. More significantly (to this discussion) they form the basis for development activities across the company. The Chairman's office, together with the Executive Committee, conducts quarterly "talent review" meetings to focus on the development of top talent in the company.

Governance and Management of TVA University

The primary drivers to establish the Tennessee Valley Authority University (TVAU) model were to achieve improved efficiencies, expand learning opportunities for employees, and provide closer integration of training to company goals.

As former CEO Crowell said, "We created an inclusive system for all education and training—the TVA University. Only when we approached it from this system perspective, could we identify areas for improvement and act on them. The systemwide perspective allowed us to stimulate much more cooperation and teamwork."

In addition a governance function was developed to manage TVA University. This governing body merged more than 40 training units, educational staffs, and training projects into a coordinated system of education, managed by TVA University, as shown in Figure 4-5.

Figure 4-5

TVA University Organization

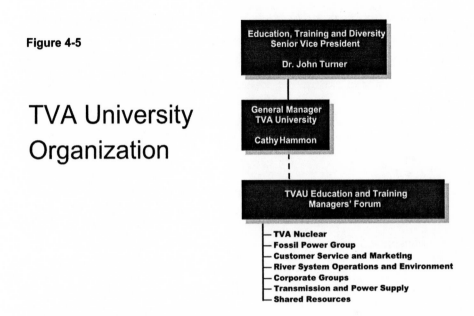

c 2001, Tennessee Valley Authority

To achieve systemwide improvements, yet support ongoing and effective education and training activities, a matrix organization was designed as the next step. Under this design, all education and training activities were considered to be part of the total TVA University system. At the same time, each training unit was to remain administratively responsible to its parent organization. A small corporate staff at Tennessee Valley Authority University was created to provide overall leadership, deal with system-wide needs, and manage the infrastructure processes necessary to support TVA University.

The position of general manager, created to put the matrix structure into operation, serves two roles—overseeing the entire TVA University system and managing the corporate university staff.

The TVA University Education and Training Managers' Forum: Create Governance for your Training Staff

In addition to involving business managers in a governance function, TVAU also created a structure to bring together all TVA training managers, This is known as the TVA Training Managers' Forum. With the General Manager of TVA as the chairperson the Training Managers Forum, its primary functions are to:

- Discuss performance issues that exist across organizations
- Identify common approaches to training solutions
- Identify common problems, opportunities to improve
- Share information, new developments, lessons learned, best practices
- Recommend programs and policies to appropriate executive bodies
- Communicate information and feedback on training issues
- Promote continuous learning in all organizations

The Training Managers' Forum has allowed TVAU learning and development professionals to seek common ground, propose joint solutions, and take part in cooperative ventures.

Governance at Cisco Systems:
An Interview with Tom Kelly,
Vice President of Worldwide Training

Q. How did the Cisco e-Learning Business Council come into existence?

Kelly. The e-Learning Business Council was initially created by a cross-functional group of five or six vice presidents who wanted to get some consistency and coherence around a multi-pronged effort in the company about e-learning. They wanted to establish a strategic convergence of all the multiple efforts that were going on in the e-learning space around the company. They started out with about five or six of us. As we started to have more and more visibility, influence and impact, it grew to about 22 people—a small number VP's of as the executive sponsors. They send director level or senior manager level people who make sure the strategy that's discussed and agreed to at the cross functional corporate level is implemented at the tactical level.

Q. Is Cisco CEO John Chambers involved in the business council?

Kelly. No. I meet with him every six to eight weeks to discuss e-learning in general, including the counsel if it's appropriate.

Q. What do you discuss?

Kelly. What's going on with e-learning. What we're doing from an internal standpoint, from an external standpoint. And what the industry is doing separate from Cisco. It's just general updating on the state of the e-learning industry, an industry that's only about three years old.

Q. Has e-learning at Cisco led to increase in market share ore retain competitive edge?

Kelly. We believe it helps retain a competitive edge. And that it has an effect on revenues. We get information out to every salesperson in the world. Every salesperson in the world has access to a communiqué, a video, a white paper—whatever—a course, a seminar online within 72 hours of its launch. It's mirrored all over the world on 175 different servers.

So the continuity of putting out information, communication, education and training consistently around the world without multiple management layers of filtering, agendas or cultural translations is huge.

Q. Has the learning function helped to lower employee turnover?

Kelly. Employee turnover is already significantly lower than the rest of the industry's, so I think it does help with retention, but hard to document because retention is so high and turnover is so low already.

Q. Has it helped to retain customers?

Kelly. We certainly believe that customer satisfaction is impacted by better trained and better informed partners as well as sales people, customer support and technical assistance. We certainly have seen positive comments from a number of our reseller partners as well as our customers. And customer satisfaction continues to increase rather dramatically.

Q. Does CEO Chambers teach a course?

Kelly. No, John attends meetings, he does company announcements, he might do a product launch. He does an awful lot of communication to the company using video, audio and slides and that information is transferred to those 175 servers all over the world. Every employee has access to the messages he sends out. It's a direct link from John to every employee.

Q. Would you say that John Chambers is a sponsor, directly or indirectly, of the Cisco e-learning business council and the work you're doing?

Kelly: Sure, you can argue that Chambers launched the e-learning industry at Comdex two years ago (1998), where he gave it legitimacy and gave it a boost that no other CEO to date has done. He is incredibly supportive of e-learning in general in the industry and that makes it a priority and a corporate initiative under his umbrella that he wants to see if not perfected, improved week to week and month to month. He's very public, he's very visible internally about e-learning. He's very public about it externally.

Q. What did Chambers say about e-learning?

Kelly. He said it was a killer application. It was the next killer application for the internet. That when it matured it would make e-mail a rounding error by comparison in size and scope and impact. And that it was the great equalizer. If you take the internet and education and combine them that will lower the barriers for individuals, companies and countries who embrace the tools and technology of e-learning.

Q. Does Mr. Chambers attend annual meetings of your learning function or other activities?

Kelly. No, he doesn't attend. He will very often if asked make a video appearance because he is on the road most of the time.

Q. How Chambers' support helped the learning function?

Kelly: His support makes it impossible to resist. You have to find ways to participate, whether you agree or not, whether you think it's as effective as classroom or not, his support forces convergence and forces participation in the project.

Chapter Summary

A governance system supported by senior management is an essential component of a corporate university or strategic learning program. Senior managers, including the CEO, can help define program goals, course curriculum, and performance measures in the early stages of development.

Afterward, once the program actually gets underway, the Chief Learning Officer can help keep senior managers informed on milestone developments, and elicit suggestions about new initiatives and improvements to the program.

Action Steps: Setting Up A Governing Board

1) Recognize that assembling a governing board is more than calling together a meeting. Key selection criteria must be outlined for the stakeholders on the governing body. The selection criteria for identifying candidates include a) demonstrate a commitment to learning and development in their area; b) represents a business unit within the organization that is experiencing rapid growth; c) is comfortable becoming a spokesperson for the education function; d) sees 'what's in it for me,' and will spend the time needed to become a senior consultant.

2) Develop an on-going relationship with senior business leaders and be proactive in suggesting how investing in education can help achieve business goals.

3) Ask how learning efforts currently align to corporate goals and propose changes for the future.

4) Propose opportunities for the governing board to learn about industry trends during meetings. Be creative and include outside experts on the agenda, for example, invite a Wall Street analyst to speak on macroeconomic issues. The board must be engaged, motivated and see their involvement as a worthwhile effort.

Lesson #4

Identify Subject Matter Experts
and build real-time links from business issues to training

▼

CHAPTER FIVE:

THE CEO AS SUBJECT MATTER EXPERT

"The problem with learning from experience is that we get the test before the lesson."

—*Alfred E. Newman*

A subject matter expert, by definition, is an individual who exhibits the highest level of expertise in performing an assigned job. Every CEO is qualified as an expert in many aspects of the company's business, even if they delegate decisions about day-to-day management of these businesses to those further down. Some CEOs have expertise in a unique business process, particularly if they played a role in discovering that process or in bringing it to market. Michael Dell, founder of Dell Computer, developed the Dell Business Model (setting forth Dell's pioneering direct-to-consumer marketing).

Research by Bain & Company several years ago on the role CEOs play in guiding their companies identified five distinct leadership models. The five approaches to CEO leadership identified by the researchers include: 1) strategy approach, focusing on creating and implementing long-term strategy; 2) human-assets approach, articulating a set of values and a corporate vision, but day-to-day management is delegated to the business units; 3) expertise approach, stressing the use of specialized knowledge to gain competitive advantage; 4) box approach, emphasizing financial and operational controls: 5) change approach, stressing organizational change and restructuring. 1

Of the five different models, the human-assets style of management is the one most supportive of employee learning. Human-assets CEOs put a lot of emphasis on career planning and programs to increase employee retention. They tend to be sensitive to employee concerns and are strong believers in employee empowerment. Most try to push decision-making closer to the people managing the businesses. About 20% of the CEOs interviewed in the study said they followed the human-assets approach in corporate governance. 2

The CEO as Thought Leader

Management style differences aside, chief executives are the de facto thought leaders of the organizations they manage. Their leadership style also gives shape and definition to management development and employee training. The goals are quite similar, regardless of CEO leadership style or type of organization: cultivating the next generation of management, recruiting and retaining the best qualified workers, and building a set of core competencies. All are designed to add increased value for the organization's major stakeholders, employees and investors.

Dr. Bob Buckman, chief executive of Buckman Laboratories, became curious about the specialty chemical company's specialized expertise in its field shortly after taking over as CEO. Who had the keys to Buckman's knowledge—the accumulated wisdom that made Buckman Laboratories unique as a company? Was it data stored in company records? On the company's mainframe computer? Was it available in a format permitting easy retrieval? Or was it, as Buckman feared, not organized at all?

As Bob Buckman says, "We recognized early on that indeed the greatest knowledge base in our company did not reside in our computer database somewhere, but was in the heads of our individual associates worldwide. In addition, this knowledge base was the most rapidly changing asset we had. It was changing continually, every moment of the day." 3

As far back as 1987, Buckman recognized the need to harness knowledge to its full advantage. People made the same mistakes over and over, costing the company millions of dollars in extra employee training time. But it was the identification of another trend—the emergence of what Buckman calls the "knowledge worker"—that gave way to the change. "Knowledge workers, unlike manufacturing workers, own the means of production," he noted. To capture that information, Buckman formed a standard operating procedure (SOP) committee that sought to quantify and store the company's knowledge. The committee—representing various departments: sales, research, production, and management—met every week to troubleshoot problems at the plant. If a chemical wasn't turning out right, the SOP committee got together and brainstormed ways to make things work. Most importantly, they documented what they had done so that future problem solvers wouldn't have to go through the process again.

"Before knowledge sharing, there was isolation between departments," explains Andrew Mohler, a quality assurance manager at Buckman Laboratories. "Once our departments started collaborating, we found that the problems were solved much faster." But the process remained difficult. It often took days, if not weeks, for the committee to solve a given manufacturing problem, document a solution, and then disseminate it to all sites by mail or fax. In order to become truly responsive to its customers' needs, Buckman Laboratories had to manage its knowledge even more efficiently.

That's where the idea of using the Internet offered a solution. In 1995, Buckman Laboratories commissioned CompuServe to create the Chemforum: an on-line meeting area where employees could post questions and receive answers within minutes. Now, an answer to a manufacturing question was minutes or seconds away instead of days or weeks. Every employee was encouraged to participate in the forum, and before long, Buckman had built a critical mass of knowledge. Nowhere was the contrast more evident than on the factory floor.

In the days before Chemforum, a uniformed operator in a hard hat and safety goggles loaded raw materials into large stainless steel or glass containers, consulting the written standard operating procedures as he went along the chemical mixing process. If a problem came up—if, say, a chemical looked wrong or didn't test properly—the operator would get on the phone and dial a supervisor, who would then consult a manual or call another executive, until the problem had been solved. After the Chemforum was installed, the operator might make the same call, but a supervisor would probably log on to the Chemforum to solicit a solution from another manufacturing location.

The Chemforum message board was subdivided into sections where messages relevant to specific topics were collected and stored in a library. In addition to collecting and managing knowledge, Buckman associates could also chat online on topics of mutual interest. While this may not sound revolutionary today, it was in 1995.

In mid 1999, Buckman Laboratories made a decision to migrate the online discussion forum from Compuserve to a company-managed intranet website to accommodate the surge in daily traffic on the network. The intranet site was given the name K'Netix, short for the Buckman Knowledge Network. Nine servers support the company's Intranet and forums were built on newsgroup-based technology using the Microsoft Internet Explorer browser. Rather than storing SOP committee material on paper, as it was a decade ago, Buckman has shifted the knowledge to an intranet.

Indeed, K'Netix has morphed into a broader technology solution that the company bills as a customer-focused system to provide instant access to the collected knowledge of all Buckman associates worldwide. The Buckman intranet does more than store and share knowledge—like the Web, it is something akin to a living organism that grows with the company's information needs.

Example of Knowledge Sharing at Buckman Laboratories

If a paper mill superintendent needed photographs of a new machine and also wanted local publicity for his or her environmental preservation award, he requested a visit from an associate from the marketing department. The marketing specialist conferred with the technical specialist who handled that account to better familiarize himself with the unique specifications of the mill. Then he or she took the necessary photographs and tapped into wide-ranging media contacts to obtain publicity for the mill. While this level of service is certainly designed to help the customer to prosper, it has benefits for the associate as well. The ability to actually visit the customer on-site, to see the operation of a paper mill or tannery or water treatment plant in action gives the associate invaluable practical information about the businesses they serve. With K'Netix®, the Buckman Knowledge Network, the company provides not only technical assistance for customers but also enables them to anticipate problems and develop a solution before any downtime occurs.

---

c 2001, courtesy of Buckman Laboratories

Success Story with K'Netix

An often-told story at Buckman helps illustrate what K'Netix can do. The managing director of Asia, based in Singapore, sent out a call for help over the bulletin boards for papermaking technologies on January 3 at 12:05 p.m. It read, "We will soon be proposing a program to an

Indonesian pulp mill. I would appreciate an update on successful recent pitch-control strategies in your parts of the world." The first response came three hours later from an associate in Memphis and included a suggestion and a reference to an academic paper on pitch control written by an Indonesian who was studying at North Carolina State University. Fifty minutes later, another associate from Canada offered his experience in solving pitch control problems in British Columbia. Shortly afterward, an associate from Sweden offered advice, and then two case studies showed up from Spain and France. An example from Memphis contributed scientific advice from the R&D team headquarters; another sent a chemical formula with specific application instructions from Mexico; and still another offered two types of pitch control programs in South Africa. In all, the original request generated over 11 replies from 6 countries, stimulating "sidebar conversations" as more and more associates logged on. All of this information, plus the demonstrated capability of the company to find quick answers to difficult problems, put the Asian managing director in position to secure a $6 million order in Indonesia.

An Early Attempt at Knowledge Management

Why and how did knowledge management become important to Buckman Laboratories? The reason is simple: it became important to Bob Buckman. He considered the idea of knowledge management before it became a buzzword in the vocabulary of the general public, but what does that mean to his customers in practical terms? It's easiest to understand the benefits to the customer of K'Netix® and the company's other knowledge transfer capabilities by describing its features: product information, technical information, and conferencing with technical specialists—instant contact with the best problem-solvers in the specialty chemical industry.

Buckman considers K'Netix to be "the greatest revolution in the way of doing business we have seen in our lifetime." He attributes the company's 250 percent sales growth over the past decade to knowledge sharing. For him, K'Netix was not a project with clearly defined goals, but "a journey with no end that has invaded the fabric of our corporation."

Buckman's personal interest in preserving his company's most precious commodity—its specialty knowledge—led him to become a self-taught expert on knowledge management—before it gained widespread recognition as a competitive tool. Buckman's early understanding of the importance of knowledge sharing in a decentralized organization made him the de facto thought leader at Buckman Laboratories.

Attracting the Best Workers

Thomas Tierney of Bain & Company sees the biggest challenge for any professional service firm, and for Bain in particular, is to attract and retain the right kind of people and to work with them to create "real-time" applied knowledge. An example of Tierney's leadership in action is the recruitment campaign he calls "Constellation Leadership" targeting the top quartile of the talent pool: nurturing them, providing incentives and creating networks to get them to talk with other stars. Says Tierney: "If we get all that right, we then can track the stars to accelerate learning throughout the system. That's where true value is created nowadays."

Another of Tierney's asset-building challenges emerges from the graying of the firm's leadership. "How do we capture and perpetuate the wisdom learned from our first-generation leaders?" he asks.

Asset building extends beyond the current roster of Bain employees. The firm's alumni program has contributed significantly to Tierney's attempts to expand the company's learning network. "We want to see Bain as a lifetime relationship that may span several careers," says Tierney. "Our alumni are 'from us,' but no longer 'of us,' you might say. They know us, how we think, what we value. But they also infuse our thinking with the richness of non-Bain experience. Obviously, with all these Bain alumni out there, we can't afford *not* to maintain positive and productive alumni relations. This also works positively against any inclination to maintain our intellectual purity."

Tierney also sees case-team staffing as an opportunity to build Bain's human assets. He maintains that promoting broad membership in practice areas helps overcome case-team myopia. "In principle," he says, "you don't want 'dedicated' thinkers because dedicated thinkers create fire walls against spreading ideas. That doesn't mean we don't nurture experts. But it does mean that we're trying to create a learning architecture where Bain people learn in a variety of contexts."

Tierney is adamant in committing Bain's case-team and firm leadership resources to flagship programs. "The consultant trainer pool will grow in proportion to the numbers we have to train," he says. "But that's a complexity issue, not a scale issue. It is and will continue to be expensive. But consider the value! Our internal data show us that our partners rank being a trainer as one of the most outstanding activities of their careers. I would never want to go to a cadre of professional trainers to do the bulk of our training. I want consultants, managers, senior partners *all* involved in training. As trainers they learn more. They become more integrated and committed to the firm's goals and values. They come back from the programs truly energized. They show their student colleagues what it means to be a committed teacher-learner! This has been my experience at Bain. This is who we are and how we succeed," adds Tierney.

Michael Dell and the Dell Business Model

The role of the CEO as Subject Matter Expert is perhaps most evident at Dell Computer. While every CEO is undoubtedly qualified as an expert in many aspects of his or her business, Michael Dell is exceptionally so. He is not only the founder of the company, but as inventor of the fundamental business model on which the company is based, he is uniquely qualified as a subject matter expert.

Dell Learning has developed an on-line training program titled The Dell Business Model. Although the contents of the actual training program are confidential, here's a peek at the basic tenants of the model as described on the Dell Computer website:

The Dell Direct Model

Dell's award-winning customer service, industry-leading growth, and financial performance continue to differentiate the company from competitors. At the heart of that performance is Dell's unique direct-to-customer business model. "Direct" refers to the company's relationships with its customers, from home PC users to the world's largest corporations. There are no retailers or other resellers adding unnecessary time and cost or diminishing Dell's understanding of customer expectations. Why are computer-systems customers and investors increasingly turning to Dell and its unique direct model? There are several reasons:

- **Price for Performance.** By eliminating resellers, retailers and other costly intermediary steps together with the industry's most efficient procurement, manufacturing, and distribution process, Dell offers its customers more powerful, more richly configured systems for the money than competitors.

- **Customization.** Every Dell system is built to order. Customers get exactly, and only, what they want.

- **Service and Support.** Dell uses knowledge gained from direct contact before and after the sale to provide award-winning, tailored customer service.

- **Latest Technology.** Dell's efficient model means the latest relevant technology is introduced in its product lines much more quickly than through slow-moving indirect distribution channels. Inventory is turned over every 10 or fewer days, on average, keeping related costs low.

The Dell Business Model (DBM) training was developed through an intensive series of interviews with the CEO. Dell spent hours recounting the evolution of the model and clarifying its basics and its subtleties. Based on those interviews, draft content was written. Michael Dell then reviewed each word of the program, sometimes rewriting sections, other times suggesting improvements or additions. The resulting program is peppered with icons called "Michael Dell Says," which allow the learner to hear from Michael on key subjects in the founder's own words. Another feature of the program is "dig downs" that allow a learner to decide to learn more by accessing supplemental materials. Today, countless tools, modules, presentations, and training programs have been derived from that single program authored by the CEO. The "Know the Net" course, a self-paced online introduction to the Internet, is another example of how Michael Dell has spearheaded learning at Dell. The course takes forty-five minutes to complete and ends with a twenty-question self-test. Employees who complete the test receive a poster proclaiming " Michael Dell Wants Everyone to Know the Net—Especially You."

When the company launched the "Know the Net" program two year later, Dell personally took a hand in reviewing the section on the company Internet strategy, once again acting as subject matter expert.

The CEO has contributed content expertise to learning modules ranging from the company history and values, through the use of technology, approaches to marketing, and the product development process, to the selection and appraisal of leadership talent.

Chapter Summary

CEOs as Subject Matter Experts have, among other things, assumed a personal role in creating a compelling business model. Furthermore they have used their leadership role to inculcate their vision throughout the organization.

Action Steps for CEOs as Subject Matter Expert

1. Encourage experiential learning. Much of the really useful information in an organization—ninety percent or more, according to

some estimates—isn't found in textbooks. It's learned on-the-job experience.

2. Develop leadership programs with real-time, real world links to important issues in the organization.

3. Understand the importance of nurturing alumni who become ambassadors for your organization.

4. Build a community around the concept you are trying to inculcate—such as Buckman's K'Netix.

5. Have fun sharing your knowledge. Michael Dell's poster says it all: Michael Wants Everyone to Know the Net—Especially You.

Lesson #5

Promote of the importance of having your CEO as faculty to celebrate and spread the culture of the organization

CHAPTER SIX:

▼

THE CEO AS TEACHER

"My only two passions are employees and customers. Because if I don't look after my employees they won't look after our customers.
—John Chambers, CEO Cisco Systems

The most visible contribution a CEO can make to a corporate education program is to lead the training themselves. Some chief executives exert a hands-on role in leadership development programs, passing on their knowledge and experience to aspiring managers. Others take part in more formal new employee orientation programs, and help initiate new hires to the organization's culture and business model.

Regardless of the setting, CEO involvement in training programs sends a powerful message to all employees about the importance of training activities. As corporations become dependent on knowledge sharing, CEOs can expect to spend more of their time teaching, coaching, and mentoring each new class of managers in the organization.

There are numerous examples of CEOs acting as teachers or learning facilitators. George David, CEO of United Technologies, co-facilitates a course in leadership at the Darden School of Business at the University of Virginia. David travels to the Darden School of Business in Charlottesville, Virginia to meet with UTC managers and exchange ideas with UTC managers enrolled in the company's Emerging Leaders Course.

Jack Welch, CEO of General Electric, is the highest profile corporate executive to take a direct role in employee training. Twice a month Welch travels to GE's Management Development Institute in Crotonville, N.Y., where he meets with GE managers. Welch teaches a 3 1/2 hour class on leadership that is offered several times a year, and has encouraged other GE top executives to also teach classes.

Jurgen Weber, CEO of Deutsche Lufthansa, the German airline company, is an active participant in the company's management development program administered by the Lufthansa School of Business, Deutsche Lufthansa's corporate university. Weber meets regularly with rising young managers taking part in management development courses, providing coaching and hands-on assistance in problem-solving exercises.

One Deutsche Lufthansa program, the *CEO Challenge*, takes place over a period of eight or nine months. Participants in the challenge are given a project of strategic importance to the company and at the end of the course they are asked to give a report to management in which they outline their observations or recommendations for making business improvements.

George David As Teacher

A key element of UTC partnership with the Darden School of Business is participation by the company's senior executives, such as Karl Krapek, president and chief operating officer of UTC, and Steve Page, president of Otis Elevator Company.

UTC company presidents are regular speakers at the Darden programs. The sessions start with remarks by the senior executive, and quickly move to an energetic Q&A on company and leadership issues. "The success of the program depends on direct links to the top leadership of the company," says Bob Harris, UTC's chief learning officer. "The support of George David and the senior management team is critical."

George David's direct involvement in establishing and supporting educational programs has had an impact throughout the corporation. In addition to launching UTC-wide programs initiated from the Corporate Office, the CEO's commitment to education has spawned a number of innovative programs in UTC's business units, broadening the capabilities of their employees. When leaders of the business units know the CEO values education, it provides a strong stimulus for them to establish education programs of their own.

The UTC division Pratt & Whitney has a computer-based program that teaches engineers and other professionals about the business impact of their activities. The Business Decision Making program is a one-week course that focuses on making decisions in the context of Pratt & Whitney's business strategies. By enhancing their financial skills, engineers are learning how to have a broader participation in the company's investment decisions. The ultimate goal is world-class financial returns.

John Cassidy, UTC's vice president for research and technology, has seen the impact of David's leadership in the technical realm. As chairman of UTC's Technical Council, which also includes the director of the corporate research center and the chief technical officers of the business units, Cassidy shares responsibility for ensuring the corporation's leadership in technology.

"Technical education is not the responsibility of the chairman," he says. "It should be the responsibility of the technical leaders. But frankly speaking, when we look at the pioneering policies and programs George has established, it causes us to think more about this—and to think more out of the box—than we would have otherwise. George has been a clear and consistent supporter of education in all forms since I've been at UTC, which has been 10 years," Cassidy adds. "He underscores a principle to which many organizations give lip service. Education is not a cost; it is an investment. George understands how various aspects of business are linked together. If you look at the cost of hiring an employee, it's $100,000 or more, including recruiting costs and executive time for campus visits and interviews. So investing in education and retaining a high percentage of employees is actually, over time, a cost saving for the enterprise. "But it also pays off in terms of morale. People see that we are investing in them," says Cassidy.

Deutsche Lufthansa's Jurgen Weber: CEO as Coach

Companies in continental Europe, like their American counterparts, have come to view training activities as integral to the success of their corporate business model. Deutsche Lufthansa AG, Germany's largest airline and an investor-owned company since 1996, became the first German company to establish a corporate university, the Lufthansa School of Business, to coordinate all company-sponsored training activities. The Lufthansa School of Business, founded in 1998, was given three broad goals as its mission: 1) aligning all Deutsche Lufthansa 's learning activities with its strategic management goals; 2) driving mental and cultural change following the reorganization of Deutsche Lufthansa in the mid-1990s; 3) serving as an internal think tank for the Deutsche Lufthansa Group of companies.

"We definitely needed to speed up the learning process because the world is changing faster and faster," says Michael Heuser, head of the business school. While Deutsche Lufthansa itself reorganized into a group of independently managed operating companies, company managers believed it was important to put training activities under control of a single training organization for the first time. "We needed a central institution that helps the entire organization learn faster than we did in the last decade," Heuser adds. Competition in the airline industry has evolved in the last decade into competition of airline alliances, requiring a greater degree of cooperation between airlines on everything from aircraft main-tenance to new employee initiation."

Deutsche Lufthansa is a founding member of the Star Alliance, an con-sortium of 13 airlines, including United Airlines, Singapore Airlines, SAS and several other major airlines. The Lufthansa School of Business facili-tates cross-company cooperation in the airline industry by building plat-forms to develop joint understanding—joint culture, and to train certain capabilities for the entire workforce.

CEO Weber, a guiding force in Deutsche Lufthansa 's transition from government ownership to public company, has played a visible and influ-ential role in the Deutsche Lufthansa School of Business. He is involved in almost every course that we run for management and young professionals. According to Heuser, Deutsche Lufthansa 's chief executive teaches leader-ship courses twice a month, and he also devotes time to developing new courses. "He spends a lot of time teaching, but what is more important is his active involvement with students during the learning process." In the Deutsche Lufthansa *CEO Challenge*, students meet regularly with the company CEO, review their progress and Weber gives them a direction on how to continue the work. "It's more than teaching," says Heuser, the manager of Lufthansa School of Business about Weber's hands-on involve-ment in teaching, "it's really coaching, meeting participants, helping them continue their work."

Lufthansa School of Business courses are modular in design, and are a combination of classroom instruction, course assignments, and learning on the job. As Heuser explains: "Our programs are modular concepts, where we teach what is going on in the business. You have 'learning phases' where you need a kind of remote atmosphere. Then you have 'transfer phases' where you need to be in the middle of the business and try to bring what you've learned into the business," adds Heuser.

Modular design brings added flexibility, as teaching (and learning) can exist side by side, independent of where the instruction takes place. At Lufthansa School of Business, the close relationship between Deutsche

Lufthansa business units and the corporate university are evident. "If instruction takes place in a classroom, the business has to come into the classroom," Heuser explains. "There are only two ways of doing this: either you bring teaching into the classroom or you bring business into the teaching."

Michael Dell's Day in a Class

At the Austin, Texas headquarters of Dell Computer Corporation, Michael Dell regularly teaches a class on the history, business model, and future of the company. He guides attendees through a structured discussion of the origins of the company and its model. He discusses fundamental values and principles, talks about how the business has evolved and how it is likely to continue evolving. The CEO is not alone on the faculty. The two vice chairmen, Kevin Rollins and Mort Topfer, also teach sections of the program, as do five other members of the executive committee. Those few top execs who don't teach right now have volunteered and are waiting their turn. "I know there are a number of companies in which the CEO plays some role in delivering training," says Dell's VP of HR, Paul McKinnon, who personally facilitates each program. "But I've never encountered a program in which the practice includes so many key executives and where the faculty consists exclusively of the top leaders of the business."

As an example, the following illustrates a typical; agenda for a two-day session.

Figure 6-1: Strategic Leadership @ Dell

Day 1

Time	Topic	Speaker
8:00–8:30	Agenda, introductions, logistics, etc.	Paul McKinnon, VP, HR
8:30–9:30	Origin of the Dell Business Model	Michael Dell, Chair/CEO
9:30–12:30 10:30–10:45 break	Strategic Thinking Process • Presentation, case study & sele cted readings (sent prior to course), teams report out, discussion • As it relates to the Dell Business Model • Q&A with Kevin	Kevin Rollins, Vice Chairman
12:30 – 1:30	Lunch	
1:30 – 2:15	Operationalizing the Model • Overview presentation - how we make it work	Kevin Rollins
2:15–2:25	Model in Transactions/Relationship Business • Presentation	Paul Bell, Senior VP

2:25–2:40	Break	
2:40 – 3:35	How Model Works in Transaction Business • Presentation and discussion	Paul Bell
3:35–4:30	How Model Works in Relationship Business • Presentation and discussion	Joe Marengi, Senior VP
4:30–5:45	Executive Selection • Selection issues – where are we? • What are we doing to improve? • Interaction around strategic selection issues	Tom Green, Senior VP
5:45–6:00	End of Day Review	Paul McKinnon
6:30–9:00	Strategic Dinner (location TBD)	

Day 2

Time	Topic	Speaker
8:00–8:15	Open Day 2	Paul McKinnon
8:15–9:45	Executive Compensation • Leveraging executive compensation • Levers and how to use: salary, bonus, options	Tom Meredith - Senior Vice President and Chief Financial Officer
9:45–10:00	Break	
10:00–11:00	Product Development for Competitive Advantage • Presentation and discussion	Carl Everett –Senior Vice - President
11:00–12:00	Driving the Customer Experience • Presentation, discussion, team activity	
12:00–1:00	Lunch	
1:00–2:30	Business Planning • Overview of Dell's performance, Dell advantage, growth engines, and the business planning approach and process	Mort Topfer

2:30–2:45	Break	
2:45–3:30	Team Presentations	Patricia - Nathan Vice President, Customer Loyalty
3:30–4:30	Customer Experience and Competitive Strategy • Lead discussion on major challenges, where we are succeeding. • Optimizing executive performance	Mort Topfer
4:30–5:00	Leadership Overview	Kevin Rollins
5:00–5:15	Course Wrap-up	Paul McKinnon

C 2001, Dell Computer Corporation

Participants in the program clearly see the value of the CEO and top execs as faculty. These are comments taken directly from the program evaluations:

"We were able to hear first hand from the OOC [Office of the Chairman] and other senior managers about strategies. We may have heard them elsewhere, but by hearing them first-hand from the source we were able to ensure consistency and filtered out any 'hallway whispers' or third party interpretations."

"History of Dell from Michael was excellent—having only been at Dell two years, understanding the history makes you bond even more with the company. I liked how Michael talked about how the mistakes Dell has made turned into good things and the company learned from the mistakes."

"We got direct exposure to the members of the OOC and other senior managers and heard directly from them about our business model and our core principles. We also got direct responses to a broad range of questions related to them."

"Please pass along my appreciation for the opportunity to participate in this program. To have the opportunity to listen to the OOC and other Senior Dell Executives made the information that much more applicable. As I have said before, one of the keys has been the opportunity to network and meet other Dell Executives and listen to concerns that they have as well. Certainly to top this off with a dinner at Michael's home was exceptional. Many thanks and I am looking forward to participation in other similar events"

"I left the program with a good understanding from Michael, Kevin, and Mort, of their expectations of me and the leadership at Dell for future success. The early presentations by Kevin, and then later by Michael, definitely set the tone and explained why we headed where we are and how our behavior needs to follow our goals."

"The background and strategic framework provides a great structural foundation for running the business and the sales process overview gave good insight into the drivers that affect the revenue generation engine."

"All the sessions by Kevin, Mort and Michael were the best. Each gave a unique perspective and all of them were packed with useful content. They really helped cement a common vision. I think most of all they were extremely motivating. I think everyone left the 2 days really pumped up."

"The most valuable session was Michael's after-dinner talk. It gave us a lot of insight into what he believes will drive the future success of the business in a way that I had not heard articulated before. It also brought a lot of credibility to our achieving our objectives, which I'd heard stated in the past. I think that this was important to hear."

"Most valuable sessions were those with Michael, Kevin, and Mort, principally because the open dialogue provided excellent insight into the Office of the Chairman's strategic thinking."

"The time commitment made by the Chairman's Office and the quality of their presentations MADE the class exceptional."

This approach—business leaders as teachers—has caught on. Another program, aimed at the director level population, now features it's own contingent of Dell VPs and directors.

Michael Dell's formal "teaching" responsibilities aren't limited to a single venue, however. Each quarter, right after meetings with Wall Street analysts discussing his company's performance, Dell invites every executive in the company to meet with him on the same subject. The CEO reviews company performance, taking time to explain key leverage points, why successes occurred, and where opportunities still exist. At every session, he's teaching the Dell Business Model.

It's worth noting that there is now a growing contingent of company's MBAs whose first exposure to Dell Computer Corporation was a presentation by Michael Dell. It's a great recruiting tool, but it also symbolizes the CEOs connection to learning. When the MBAs meet periodically during their first few months on the job, the CEO is often there in his teaching role, helping to accelerate assimilation into the company.

CEO as Teacher-Learner

Some chief executives "teach" by setting the agenda for learning, as opposed to teaching a course. These CEOs encourage other senior managers to take on teaching roles, but may limit their teaching duties because other responsibilities impose limits on their available time.

At Bain & Company, the management consulting firm, the choice of faculty for formal training programs emerges from former CEO Thomas Tierney's vision of Bain as a community of "teacher-learners." Tierney himself serves as a trainer in three or four programs a year, including New

Partner Training and New Manager Training. In addition to preparation time, he commits a week of his schedule annually to delivering training.

Tierney's commitment to learning extends beyond thinking about and promoting the learning function. He figures prominently on training agendas, usually sharing his insights into the state of the firm, its values, performance, and direction. He also actively and regularly participates in training sessions for which he is not a trainer, especially those that focus on partner professional development and building the firm's intellectual capital.

When the Bain Virtual University (BVU) was in the concept stage, Tierney volunteered to be a presenter in one of the first videos offered on the BVU prototype. In the most current version of the intranet learning center, Tierney provides a videotaped welcome to new employees as part of the on-line orientation program. "Tom also spearheaded the development of our 25th Anniversary CD-ROM," says Steven Tallman, former vice president of training. "He appears throughout. It was so successful that we have reconfigured the program to appear as an interactive 'Bain History, Values, and Culture' module on the BVU."

Tierney has a reputation at Bain for being an avid learner. As a newly promoted junior vice president in the San Francisco office, he enrolled in a series of external courses in selling skills and time management. "The pressure to immerse completely in client work is immense, especially for a new partner," he remembers. "At a time when the firm focused primarily on professional development below the VP level, I felt strongly that my own investment in my capabilities and capacity was critical."

Keeping a personal diary of questions and thoughts is part of Tierney's daily discipline. He often distills these thoughts and shares them as part of his career advice to managers at New Manager Training.

For most of his professional career, Tierney has maintained one-year, five-year, and ten-year goals, which he now records in his palm pilot and to which he refers regularly.

Bain's learning strategy reflects Tierney's embrace of the teacher-learner model. In every "learning moment," each party is both a teacher and a learner, Tierney suggests. He compares Bain's learning model to apprenticeship-based medieval guilds. "As with the medieval guilds—take the goldsmiths, for example—in this business you're always teaching someone junior to yourself," he observes. "At the same time, you're learning from people more experienced than you. That person may be on your team, somewhere else in your office in the Bain network, or a client. Learning isn't just hierarchy-based. Everyone learns from everyone else. It goes in all directions—top-down, lateral, you name it. And we make sure it happens that way."

Teacher-learners, according to Tierney, share several characteristics:

- They actively engage in teaching, probing, and learning—all going on simultaneously.

- They demonstrate caring for their colleagues, making intellectual and emotional connections in and beyond their circle of peers.

- They neutralize their "data-receiving filters." Tierney explains, "Teacher-learners keep their receiver-transmitters on. They possess a 'child's mind,' as Zen masters put it. They don't presuppose, they listen. They tend not to superimpose their assumptions on a 'listening opportunity.'"

- Teacher-learners nurture bandwidth capacity. They relate to many people from different backgrounds, experience, thinking types, values, maturity levels, incomes, and positions.

- They have a learning *content* focus as well as a *process* focus. That is, they reflect on *what* they have learned and *how* they learn. They not only pursue what they can learn in an interaction, but afterward also ask, "What have I learned about learning? What should I explore now to enrich my own learning as a result of this interaction?"

- Teacher-learners are made, not born. A teacher-learner profile, Tierney asserts, is the product of role models, parents, friends, experiences, a faith community, and other institutions.

Bain organizes learning based on the consequences of this teacher-learner approach for strategy consulting. As a result, systems and relationships for learning at Bain are organized around Tierney's vision of a community of teacher-learners. For example, Tierney asks, "How do you organize for learning in a flatter learning structure? How do you design your plant—your facilities, even your floor plan—for learning? How do you organize case teams? How do you set up and manage client interactions for learning? What are the implications for recruiting? That is, how do you go about hiring people who are both teachers and learners? What is the role of the corporate center? What is the role of individual Bain offices in managing their own learning and in sharing lessons learned across the worldwide network (or, how do you *learn locally* and *teach globally*)?" But the most difficult question to answer, Tierney suggests, is "How do you sustain a teacher-learner approach in a context of rapid obsolescence of learning?"

The Bain Training Organization

"The important thing to remember is that training is at the center of the body. It's not just an appendage 'out there.' That means that training is linked—it's fully integrated—with other organizational components, such as performance reviews, staffing, compensation, and reward systems."

—Tom Tierney

In 1998, Bain was ready to revamp its training strategy. Distractions set off by a corporate restructuring in 1990 had long since been eliminated. "In the late 80s, we were literally fighting for our survival. We had layoffs in our Boston and London offices. This was very painful because of the fierce interpersonal loyalties in our 'tribal' culture. And this cutback was literally on the eve of our flagship Associate Consultant Training program, which we decided to go forward with. But as far as other program budgets were concerned, we were somewhat constrained," says Tierney.

By the mid-90s, Bain had achieved full fiscal and organizational recovery. Revenues were up substantially and the firm reoccupied its former position as a prized recruiter on business school campuses. The firm expanded both in numbers and complexity. Headcount edged up, new offices opened, and Bain made available to clients new industry capabilities. "We had turned the corner," Tierney recalls. "With all the talk about 'learning organizations,' we were convinced we weren't reaching our full potential. So we thought we had better take stock of where we stood as a learning organization."

The first step was to conduct a learning audit. Says Tierney, "Since we recommend audits as a way of assessing a client's benchmark status, we took a similar approach to revamp the Bain training organization. Tierney created the Worldwide Training Advisory Group, composed of five senior partners: one partner each from North America, Asia, and Europe; the head of Bain's Strategy Practice; and the partner for VP Professional Development. This group would ensure quality decision-making, buy-in and implementation of a new training organization. First convened in 1997, the advisory group met quarterly to review results and monitor the implementation of new training initiatives. The group also presented Tierney with business plans for the training organization, which addressed 1) Bain's training operations and short- and long-term needs, 2) key milestones and 3) quick wins. "We basically became consultants to ourselves, "Tierney admits. "That doesn't come easily to client-focused strategy consultants. When our clients come to us asking for help, we think it's a sign of strength. When *we* do it, it's a different story. But given what we knew about learning organizations and given our back-of-the-envelope hunches about our own training function, we had to ask ourselves, 'What would an outside strategy firm say about learning in our organization? How are our vital signs doing? What is our prognosis? Are we in danger of eventually failing to thrive intellectually, even as our business continues to thrive and expand?'"

Specifically, the Bain Training Business Plan defines a learning vision, a master training plan for the next 3-5 years and helps identify a number of informal learning opportunities.

The learning audit compiled data from a variety of sources: company interviews across all levels and positions; competitor analysis; surveys of corporate and local office training programs, program performance records (costs, program feedback scores and organizational impact, and participation trends); and industry perspectives on current and developing learning technologies, *e.g.,* e-learning, extranets and collaborative learning.

Reviewing the output of the worldwide learning audit, Tierney quickly concluded that while individual problem-solving and analytical modules were highly effective, Bain was less effective at training consultants to move the client to action. "From a training perspective, we were dropping the ball on one of our fundamental core corporate values," Tierney adds.

Drawn primarily from among Bain's own strategy and industry experts, trainers are recruited from among the firm's best thinkers and peak performers. "For faculty, we draw upon the top 20 percent of high-performing consultants," Tierney emphasizes. "Being named a trainer is a much sought-after honor." Trainers for flagship programs usually occupy the level immediately above that of the students. For example, faculty for Associate Consultant Training are picked from the worldwide pool of consultants. Similarly, managers function as team leaders at New Consultant Training, and so on.

In consultation with a small cadre of internal training specialists, Bain program directors oversee a process of rigorous design, module preparation, and train-the-trainer workshops. This approach squares with Bain's principle of valuing training as the keystone of the company's strategy for building its human assets. Bain considers contributing to those assets as a faculty member not only an honor, but also a critical step in the consultant's professional development and career path.

The Bain Virtual University

The conclusions of Bain's learning audit reflected the realities of the new economy and the demands of adult learning. "Doing business in the new economy," Tierney explains, "convinced us that we had to reduce the learning cycle time. And we also knew that our learner population required that we customize training for individual needs and learning styles."

The awareness of these needs led Bain to evaluate emerging training technologies that would provide instant desktop access to the company's training resources from anywhere in the Bain system, 24 hours a day.

Bain Virtual University (BVU) was one of the conclusions arrived at in the Bain Learning Audit. The BVU is an intranet-based learning system that pushes the company's envelope of learning beyond the constraints of traditional, formal training programs to the independence of customized, self-managed learning. Essentially, the BVU answered a business need and it fit with the Bain culture.

Launched in 1999, the BVU was designed to provide instant desktop access to the best of Bain's thinking and thought leaders on strategy, case-team management, and client development. Employing audio and video streaming, linked spreadsheets, and hypertexts, BVU's training modules are packaged in a variety of formats to match Bain employees' diverse learning styles. As a virtual on-line multimedia campus, the BVU enables Bain team members worldwide to manage their own learning at their own pace. It provides customized learning by isolating skills critical to specific client work and a consultant's development skill plan.

A valued feature of the BVU is its link to Bain's proprietary research site, which provides comprehensive external information and analysis on industries, companies, the economy, and business trends. The BVU serves as both a training forum and a reference tool. It is a key element of the Bain vision to be the premier place to learn how to create value in business.

Bain's practice of involving management in formal training carries over to the BVU on at least two fronts. First, the worldwide partner group adopted the BVU as one of the firm's most strategic priorities. Second, key senior consulting and administrative staff contributed modules or participated in user testing in the BVU's inaugural edition. For example, an interactive module on Bain's history, values, and culture features more than 50 video portraits of senior people sharing their experiences of working at Bain. BVU organizers even tapped Orit Gadiesh, Bain's chairman, to contribute a video module on Bain's core values.

Most of the BVU's more than 200 instructional modules are offered in a standard presentation format. Each of these modules is a web-based slide presentation that may be viewed on-line or downloaded in PowerPoint for editing and printing. Other modules use a video format to capture live presentations featuring senior management experts. In these, a video appears in one window while synchronized slides, sound, and script support the speaker's message. Similar to videotape, the presentation may be stopped, paused, or scanned for specific information. BVU also boasts over 25 interactive computer-based tools that train users on specific tasks. This format leverages Bain training resources by reducing the need for live, stand-up instruction. Also, a battery of BVU templates guides users in completing both common and complex calculations and tasks. This format leverages Bain training resources by reducing the need for live, stand-up instruction.

Training the Trainers at STMicroelectronics

STMicroelectronics (formerly known as SGS-Thomson) is an electronics manufacturer with operations in more than 20 countries. Like any global company, STMicroelectronics must deal with problems generated by misunderstandings about customs of the various local cultures in which it works. To help ST maintain a common corporate culture at the technical, managerial and ethical levels, while adapting itself to the practices of local markets, the company has developed a multicultural training strategy. This strategy is embedded in courses offered by ST University, the company's corporate university created in 1994.

ST University was founded to reinforce the importance of developing core competencies and professional certification. Since its inception STU has trained more than 6,000 employees and certified about 150-plus internal trainers from the ranks of company management. Consistent with the principle that "ST trains ST," a corps of 350 speakers and formally certified trainers, including senior executives, participate in every learning program. Figure 6-2 shows how the "ST trains ST" model functions at the organization.

STMicroelectronics:
ST Trains ST Model

- Stage 1: A 3-day facilitation course covering key topics such as "how to manage a classroom"
- Stage 2: A 3-day "Train the Trainer" course. Course applies skills learned in the first stage
- Stage 3: Participants teach under the supervision of an ST University staff member.

  Once these stages are successfully completed, the participant is certified as an "ST University Associate Trainer"

Figure 6-2

During different management cycles, ST University conducts classes in such areas as new-hire orientation, strategy, marketing, finance, return on net assets, and economic value added. At the end of the course, ST University will invite a speaker, sometimes a senior executive, to make an informal presentation followed by a question-and-answer session. Sometimes the executive will give feedback on a trainee team's presentation. The executives, who participate on a rotating basis, have shown great enthusiasm for participating in these sessions, a testament to their desire to create a true learning organization.

CEO Pasquale Pistoria addresses company trainees through training videos and live video conferences. In addition, key executives such as the Total Quality corporate VP , group VP; corporate financial controller, and key information technology officers are regularly involved as speakers in ST University's programs to communicate and explain the company's values and to clarify key company trends in finance and new technologies. When ST University first opened, the company's managers had a widespread, pressing need to better understand finance. As a result the CFO and key financial people such as company controllers helped organize ST University's first program. The very first speakers at ST University were key financial experts from the corporate level, a product group and manufacturing.

Pushing the LATCH and
Gold Standards Campaigns at STMicroelectronics

CEO Pistorio says he does "not teach so much or enough in specific courses due to time constraints," but he involves himself with learning programs as needed. The best example of Pistorio's commitment to teaching and learning occurred in 1992. At the time, a TQEM audit revealed a pressing need to upgrade the skills of the company's employees in terms of teamwork, communication, leadership, motivation, and recognition.

Knowing that he needed to train his workforce quickly, Pistorio immediately prepared himself and his top staff so that they could teach what was needed. By teaching, Pistorio and his executives also learned how to improve themselves in the areas they were teaching. In Pistorio's words, "the culture of the company is driven by the CEO. However, if the CEO dictates 'go and do it!' nothing will really happen. If, on the contrary, the CEO practices it, as does everybody else does in the hierarchy and in the organization, then the culture is easier to establish throughout the company." Each level of the organization then taught the next level below it, with lessons flowing from the CEO to the most junior employees.

The initiative, called LATCH (short for Learn, Apply, Teach, Check), trained 28,000 employees over four years and diffused common values across the organization. The successful effort exemplified Pistorio's belief that "if any organization wants to transform itself into a learning organization, it cannot be done without the CEO religiously practicing, day after day, the behaviors needed to inculcate the organization.

When there was a growing market for commodity integrated circuits and STMicroelectronics needed to improve its position in commodity products, ST launched an extensive promotion and manufacturing campaign called "Gold Standards." As part of the "Gold Standards" campaign, CEO Pistorio and Alain Dutheil, VP of strategic planning and human resources, decided to immediately train ST's sales force on servicing commodity products. Pistorio and Dutheil asked ST University to organize in short order a training session for 50 sales people. This was accomplished in only three weeks due to ST University's efforts to rapidly network with people from the product, sales, and manufacturing divisions. ST University tapped 20 internal experts to teach and CEO Pistorio showed his personal commitment by being the training program's first speaker, explaining the different product families to the sales force and reminding them of the importance of their products.

Chapter Summary

CEO participation in learning activities is the single most important success factor in world-class training development programs. A survey of 100 corporate university deans by Corporate University Xchange identified five attributes of corporate university programs achieving success in meeting their business objectives. These CEOs don't delegate responsibility for corporate learning. Rather, they are active participants.

- The CEO is personally involved in training activities. Corporate University Xchange research has found that the CEO and company president spend an average of 1 1/2 days per month facilitating learning. They participate in "Work-Out" or idea exchange sessions with employees, as well as preside at orientation sessions for new employees.

- The CEO identifies learning goals for the organization, including "stretch" goals that include the percentage of work time employees should devote to skills improvement and preparation for the next job.

- The CEO enlists the support of external learning partners, such as customers, suppliers and academic institutions to help sponsor formal learning programs.

- The CEO publicly acknowledges the importance of continuous learning in achieving marketplace success. The CEO helps get the message out, both internally to employees, and externally to major stakeholders through annual reports, press releases, shareholder meetings and meetings with Wall Street analysts.

Teaching is the most visible way a CEO can demonstrate support for learning. Chief executive officers show their commitment to learning in many different ways: by teaching a leadership course, by coaching young managers and guiding them through a training course, by taking a speaking role at a leadership development conference.

CEOs show their support for learning even when they are not teaching but acting as the de facto chief learning officer of their organization. This translates into considerable time managing the intellectual capital of their organizations and developing the next generation of leaders.

Action Steps: CEO as Teacher

1. Think of business managers as partners in corporate learning. When you put learners in control and they learn "on the job," you are bringing business into teaching.

2. Create a structured program to train Subject Matter Experts on how to facilitate a training program. "ST trains ST" became the company mantra for business leaders as they became involved as teachers.

3. Involve the CEO and governing board in identifying learning goals for the organization.

4. Publicize leaders who become teachers.

5. Showcase "Learning CEO" to your CEO. Share examples of how CEOs (especially from competitive firms) are involved as teachers. CEOs learn from their peers.

Lesson #6

**Profile CEOs in your company's industries
that operate as "Learning CEOs."
Top management learns best from their peers.**

CHAPTER SEVEN:

▼

THE CEO AS LEARNER

"The ultimate competitive advantage lies in an organization's ability to learn and to rapidly transform that learning into action."

—*Jack Welch, CEO, General Electric*

CEOs who teach a course understand the unique bond—the synergy—that occurs between teacher and student. Because of the dynamics going on in the American economy, and throughout the world, organizations have to discover new ways of learning. In a literal sense, CEOs are always learning, because they cannot lead effectively without frequent interaction with managers who make the day-to-day decisions affecting strategy, customers, product development and many other things too numerous to mention.

Some CEOs help create an environment for learning by teaching a course; mastering the subject matter, standing before a class, forging a connection between teacher and learner. Steven R. Covey gets to the heart of the issue in his book, *The 7 Habits of Highly Effective People* when Covey discusses the sixth habit—synergy. He says: "Synergy tests whether teachers and students are really open to the principle of the whole being greater than the sum of the parts." Good teachers learn as much from their students as they pass on in the form of instruction.

Chief executives have multiple opportunities to stress the value of learning. By stressing the importance of learning to maintain job skills and support the enterprise, the CEO is the de facto chief education officer. In the broadest sense, the chief executive can help create a nurturing environment for learning by acting as a role model for others to follow. Thomas Tierney, former CEO of Bain & Company, suggests that Bain benefits from its learning strategy "by guaranteeing client success achieved by high-quality teacher-learners sharing their insights globally in a timely way."

Tierney has a reputation at Bain for being an avid learner. As a newly promoted junior vice president in the San Francisco office, he enrolled in a series of external courses in selling skills and time management. For most of his professional career, Tierney has maintained one-year, five-year, and ten-year goals, which he now records in his electronic organizer to which he refers regularly. His colleagues have observed him deeply engrossed in his notebook during flights to Bain's offices. "There is something about travel. Perhaps it's the feeling that you're suspended in time, in between places that anchor you," Tierney reflects. "I think it's a great chance to revisit my own development plan. It's an opportunity for me to be 'self-ish'—not selfish, but 'self-ish' in the sense that I can focus on my own personal and professional growth—how to be a better husband and parent, how to be a better CEO, how to juggle the two, where I've succeeded, where I need to grow more."

Client success stories. Bain's strategic approach to learning allows the firm to provide what may be its most valued commodity: customized strategies fully implemented for each client. The BVU is the chief tool for enabling this customization by providing access to a portfolio of tools and concepts that consultants can adapt to both traditional and innovative applications.

Global Integration. Bain's learning strategy pools the highest-quality resources across the firm to determine the canon of the best ways to create value in business and how to transfer that knowledge most effectively to each member of the Bain worldwide community. "We do this in a variety of contexts and cultures. But the fact is, we learn as one firm. Embedded in all our training programs and other learning activities," Tierney stresses, "are our shared values and culture of value addition and results, the primacy of the client, and concern for each member of the team."

Accelerated learning cycles. Flexibility has been built into the Bain learning system, from its intranet-based Knowledge Management systems to Capability Workshops for Bain Partners, such as e-commerce seminars. "Access to knowledge experts and distilled insights and cases enables us to cut through red tape to roll out workshops for specific audiences," Tallman notes. "And our access to case-team staffing data and the organization of administrative oversight and program coordination dramatically shrinks a workshop's time to market."

The Bain Approach to Learning

Interpersonal skills. Formal and informal training is designed to reinforce Bain's collaborative approach among team members and with clients. Accordingly, at Bain, as elsewhere, the learning context is as important as the learning content. For example, at formal programs like Associate Consultant Training, team skills are taught and experienced in a team setting, using real-life case histories. The learning unit at most programs is a team of five to six students led by a trainer-instructor. Also, collaborative team behaviors and client skills occupy a prominent position in all major program curricula.

Employee loyalty. Bain has experienced increased rates of employee retention and higher levels of employee satisfaction in the last five years; to a great extent, this is attributed to learning opportunities at the firm.

Tierney comments, "We hire people because of their intelligence and intellectual curiosity. We would be crazy not to reward that curiosity with challenging work and ready access to knowledge, experts, and mentors. We ask incredibly bright people to work very hard, but they get energized by the prospect of learning so much from so many in so brief a time."

Alumni relations. Bain alumni leverage their experience at the firm to be successful general managers and CEOs in their own right. "At our many yearly Bain alumni gatherings throughout the world," Tierney maintains, "I hear one former colleague after another tell how their most memorable experiences at Bain derive from what they learned—and how they learned—at one of our programs, like New Consultant Training, or through a mentoring relationship with a Bain manager or partner. And this positive feeling towards Bain—a vivid and positive 'remembrance of things past,' if you will—makes alumni one of our best sources of new client development."

Brand recognition. Bain's approach to Knowledge Management frequently lands it on the Internet and in the pages of newspapers and business periodicals, such as The Harvard Business Review and Financial Times.

Project ownership. "Both in our formal programs and in less formal training on the case-team level, we organize learning using an apprenticeship model," Tallman explains. "We are in the experience acquisition and application business, primarily through mentor-apprentice relationships. Everyone on the case team gets to add value to solving a client problem. The result is, when we make a recommendation to a client, everyone on the team can see how he or she contributed to the team's—and ultimately, the client's—success."

Professional growth. Tallman asserts that being a trainer at a Bain program is one of the best ways to learn the consultant's job. "You have to be regarded as an expert to qualify as a trainer in the first place," he says. "But when you have to write a module, digest the material to be able to train it, or be prepared to respond to students' questions, you don't take any of your competence for granted. You end up asking, 'Just why do we do it this way? How can I say this in the clearest way possible? How can I best engage intelligent and curious people in learning this tool? How does my experience provide color to the subject matter?' The whole teacher role pushes you to a higher level of consultant virtuosity." According to Tallman, over 15 percent of Bain's worldwide staff annually serve as trainers in the firm's formal training programs.

Michael Dell Sets an Example

Michael Dell of Dell Computer is a CEO who guides his company's short-term and long-term vision by gathering vast amounts of data, including the thousands of phone calls daily from Dell customers. These comments are categorized and organized for review. Maintaining close ties with customers serves two objectives at Dell Computer: managers become sensitized to the voice of the Dell customer; customer queries or suggestions often lead to new product ideas. As a result of calls from numerous customers, Dell was one of the first computer manufacturers to distribute small, powerful, notebook computers.

The computer manufacturer's founder is always talking about what he learns from at least three important sources: employees, outsiders, and customers—especially customers. The stories find their way into speeches and presentations that he routinely makes to his leadership team. When a Dell customer needed help getting employees to improve computer skills—and, in turn, raise the company's own productivity—the company asked for a way to make it easier and less expensive for their employees to purchase home PCs.

Dell designed an online order site for purchase of home PC's and the customer offered employees incentives such as free software, printers, extended warranties, and interest-free loans. In the first four months of the program, 6,000 employees—more than 30 percent of the customer's U.S. workforce—purchased Dell Dimension desktop or Latitude notebook computers for home use. When Michael Dell repeated the story, he emphasized what his company brought to the problem, and how much we had learned about the solution. Dell has since established similar employee-purchase programs for more than 50 other customers.

Another example goes back to 1992. Michael Dell heard an idea from a customer that may seem obvious today, but was unheard of then. "One of our customers came up with the idea of preloading software on our hard disk," said Dell in a *PC Week* article that year. "That's the kind of innovation that will help us capitalize on our greatest growth opportunity and listening to our customers gave us a two-year edge," adds Dell.

Dell Computer ran with the idea, offering installed software on pre-configured PCs. The strategy was hugely successful, and the CEO featured this customer-based learning scenario as the basis for advertising that year.

Perhaps the most wide-ranging example of the CEO as learner is the Customer Experience Initiative. The foundation of the initiative, as articulated by the chairman, is a simple one: Because of its direct sales model, Dell Computer is in direct contact with hundreds of thousands of customers every day. Each one of those interactions is an opportunity to learn how to serve the customer better. Here's how Michael Dell introduced the program in a message to all employees:

Dear Colleague:

Today marks a significant occasion at Dell as we launch a vitally important global, strategic initiative that we believe will drive our growth for years to come and help ensure that the tremendous momentum we've established in recent years continues through the next decade. As the scale and tone of today's "Chairman's Meeting" suggests, the focus on this initiative will be particularly important. In fact, it will be one of the most critical team efforts in our history.

The initiative is called the Customer Experience, and its mission is simple: leverage the direct model to deliver the best possible customer experience across all points of contact with Dell. That experience is crucial to our goal of building and sustaining customer loyalty and maximizing Dell's share of current and new markets.

More than any other company in our industry, Dell is positioned to provide the highest quality experience to keep our customers coming back year after year. After all, our direct-to-the-customer business model puts us in touch with thousands of people daily who tell us what they want and need. We take responsibility for the full "experience chain," from order and delivery through installation to service and support, giving us maximum opportunity to deliver the satisfaction level our customers want.

At the heart of the Customer Experience initiative is the support and involvement of every Dell employee. In our meetings today, I will be asking each of you to make support of the Customer Experience your top business priority every day and in every task you perform, whether it's ensuring that orders are entered correctly, completing a credit application promptly, or whatever work you do at Dell. There isn't any function in our organization that does not in some way touch the customer, and no situation where we cannot make individual contributions that will enhance the customer experience.

This initiative represents a tremendous opportunity for our company and for each of us as employees. I hope you share in the enthusiasm for this program, and keep in mind that the customer's experience is only as positive and satisfying as each one of us makes it in the work we do every day.

Sincerely,
Michael Dell

c 2001, courtesy of Dell Computer Corporation

The message had great credibility because it echoed a view toward learning from the customer that employees had come to expect to hear from the boss. When asked that very day what employees could do right away, the CEO replied: "Think like a customer. Challenge yourself to enhance the overall customer experience by working with each other to meet the needs of the customer. Continually ask yourself how you would like to be treated, and what you could do to make the Dell customer experience extraordinary. Learn from the customer. If we each do this, our rewards will be great, our customers will remain loyal, and our jobs will be easier. We will continue to lead the industry."

Michael Dell is also a voracious learner from other sources outside of Dell. He's everywhere on the Internet, grabbing new ideas and passing them on to folks inside of Dell. As in many companies, books and articles get circulated routinely for review and discussion; but when the Executive Committee of the company meets, it's likely that one of the authors of those ideas will be present to dialog directly with the company's top management. The CEO quotes liberally from those conversations, not only infusing the organization with what he has learned, but usually creating a run on the author's works also as his team strives to keep up.

In an excerpt from his book *Direct From Dell,* Michael Dell described another deliberate, systemic learning process for himself and his top management:

> In a direct business like ours, you have, by definition, a relationship with customers. But beyond the mechanisms we have for sales and support, we have set up a number of forums to ensure the free flow of information with the customer on a constant basis.
>
> Our Platinum Councils, for example, are regional meetings—in Asia-Pacific, Japan, the United States, and Europe—of our largest customers. They meet every six to nine months; in the larger regions, there's one for the information executives—the CIO types—and then there's one for the technical types.

In these meetings, our senior technologists share their views on where the technology is heading and lay out roadmaps of product plans over the next two years. There are also breakout sessions and working groups in which our engineering teams focus on specific product areas and talk about how to solve problems that may not necessarily have anything to do with the commercial relationship with Dell. For example, is leasing better than buying? Or, how do you manage the transition to Windows NT? Or, how do you manage a field force of notebook computers?

People in businesses as dissimilar as Unilever and ICI can learn from each other because, amazingly, they have very similar problems when it comes to PCs. And we send not only our top technologists and engineers but also the real engineers, the people who usually don't get out to talk to customers because they're too busy developing products. All of our senior executives from around the company participate. I spend three days at each of them.

When Michael Dell talks about what he is learning, he doesn't just quote authors and analysts. Much of what he shares he learns from employees. Most companies have "open door" policies. So does Dell Computer. But at this high-tech giant, the "open e-mail" policy is more effective. The company's "be direct" philosophy means that anyone who has the information may get a direct inquiry from the CEO and the chance to support his learning. Through that vehicle, everyone in the company has direct access to the CEO. For example, Dell sets up periodic lunch meetings with groups of employees selected and invited at random. If an employee doesn't happen to get picked for a brown bag lunch, that doesn't mean she or he won't be talking with the CEO. One of his habits is to walk the halls, dropping in on employees to ask about what they are doing, what they are hearing and what they think he should know. It's a good management technique; it is also a learning strategy.

Michael Dell's approach to his own learning is deliberate, but it's also very natural.

At executive conferences, for example, which include group working sessions, Dell—in contrast to senior executives at many other companies—is eager to participate and learn right along with the teams. And when Dell Learning launches a new on-line tool, it's a safe bet that the CEO will be among the first to use it.

Michael Dell's views are widely shared by the leadership team. One of the company's sales VPs Susan Larson was asked what advice she had for employees as they continue to build successful careers with Dell. Here's her response.

> I can offer three items as advice:
>
> 1. Focus: Employees should see projects through to completion. They should deflect distractions that waste time. Employees should do the right thing, do it right the first time, and then move on.
>
> 2. Always try to learn more about the business from others. We can all learn from peers, supervisors and employees in other areas of the company. Additionally, employees shouldn't be afraid to take a lateral career move if it means enhancing their skill set.
>
> 3. Employees should take it upon themselves to read more about things that interest them, go to seminars, network with peers and other professionals. Another very valuable way to develop great skills is to volunteer with community organizations. In other words, employees should invest in themselves."

Because learning organizations exist, by definition, within a corporate culture, they take their cue from senior management. The path to formation of a learning organization, and a change in employee behavior, begins with strong support from the CEO and senior management. If the CEO wants it to happen, he or she can create the right incentives for a learning organization to take root.

Chapter Summary

CEOs who are committed to the idea of continuous advancement and improvement of professional skills act as role models for their organizations. They apply the same approach to learning that they employ in day-to-day business decisions. An example is Bain & Company's CEO, Thomas Tierney, who put this idea in to practice by creating a Bain Academy where Bain's management consultants apply the insights gleaned from consulting assignments to Bain's own training and development.

CEO involvement in the learning process is key to creating a learning culture or a learning organization—an organization where employees share observations and best practice ideas across business units. Learning organizations promote information sharing through team learning and personal mastery of critical skills. The learning organization, much like the modern corporation, is in the process of continually re-inventing itself, searching for new ideas. A learning organization is always in the process of being constructed—the job is never completely finished.

Action Steps: CEO as Learner

1. Profile CEOs in your company's industry that operate as a Learning CEO

2. Learn from your customers. What can you suggest in the way of products/services that are the result of customer input?

3. Develop your network of training directors and share best practices in learning new skills, *i.e.* e-learning, vendor selection management and customer relationship management.

Lesson #7

Encourage your CEO to be
the Chief Spokesperson for Learning.

---▼---

Chapter Eight

The CEO as Marketing Agent for Learning

"ST University is not only a tool of promotion for the human resources of the company, but also it is a powerful vehicle to extend learning to our customers, suppliers and members of the community in which we operate."
—*Pasquale Pistorio, CEO, ST Microelectronics*

As corporate universities evolve from traditional training departments to enterprise-level systems fostering knowledge sharing, senior management support is a critically important success factor. Top management involvement and commitment sends a powerful message throughout the organization about the importance given education and training activities. In fact, no education program can survive for long without CEO endorsement and continued support.

Education and training activities will remain front burner issues as long as companies empower their employees. A decentralized, "flattened-out" organization needs better-trained employees and a continuous commitment to learning. Because authority is decentralized, it's imperative that managers are expertly trained.

Senior managers are well aware of the additional skills required of their employees. Most are supportive of training efforts that help them meet strategic goals. Some CEOs are so supportive of learning activities that they see themselves as the "public face" of their corporate university or company-sponsored learning program. They believe their role is to embody their organization's learning principles personally. Essentially they evolve to become the chief marketing agent for learning.

CEO level support doesn't just occur internally, within the organization. A survey by Corporate University Xchange of 175 corporate university deans revealed that 57 percent of the publicly traded companies talk about the contribution of their education and training strategy in the company annual report. CEOs also discuss the contribution of company-sponsored education programs in annual shareholder meetings and in meetings with securities analysts. Figure 8-1 shows three examples of how the company's commitment to learning is profiled in the annual report.

Figure 8-1 Corporate Universities in the Company Annual Report

Conoco's 1998 Annual Report:

"Under the umbrella of "Conoco University" a wide range of programs has been designed to create and sustain a continuous learning environment with Conoco. This benefits the company and responds to skill gaps identified by the staffing and development processes.

Conoco University addresses a variety of critical development challenges, ranging from enhancing business literacy skills to first line supervisor training to developing visionary leaders at the executive level.

Conoco's performance management process integrates business plans with the pursuit of individual goals. Inherent in the process is accountability for not only achieving results, but also doing so in a way that supports our core values and enables employees to develop new skills. Underpinning the process is a variety of reinforcement tools that support achievement and development."

Cox Communication's 1998 Annual Report:

"One of the programs enabling employees to more quickly and effectively develop skills required for success is Cox University, which was launched in 1998. This online, intranet-based training platform combines accessibility, convenience and time effectiveness to provide employees with numerous self-guided learning opportunities. In CU's first year, more than 2,000 employees used it to learn subjects ranging from Microsoft Office applications to **Cox@Home** installation procedures. The launch of a **Cox@Home** sales tool on CU helped increase sales by 147 percent in only one month! With a host of learning opportunities available at their fingertips, employees are advancing their skills and their careers, while giving Cox a competitive advantage in the marketplace."

Walking the Talk

Thomas Tierney, Michael Dell, Pasquale Pistorio, and other prominent CEOs are corporate leaders who act as public spokesmen for learning in their organizations. Thomas Tierney of Bain & Company unequivocally embraces his role as "Chief Learning Champion." To him, this means being a frequent contributor to business journals, commenting on Bain's business strategy as a management consulting firm, but also on trends in learning and knowledge management. Internally, it is not uncommon for Tierney to send e-mails to the entire firm announcing a new Bain Virtual University program or other key learning initiative.

As Tierney says: "I see myself as a 'public face' of Bain on view both within the company and in the business community at large," he maintains.

"That means that I make it my business to appear on the front lines. It means that I go public in my words and actions."

Tierney also believes firmly that it is his role to try to persuade other Bain leaders to be public boosters of Bain's learning strategy and active partners in its implementation. He actively encourages other Bain partners to disseminate Bain insights and success stories in print and through televised interviews. Combining his roles as faculty member and marketing agent, Tierney is also a guest lecturer at Harvard Business School on the management of professional service firms.

Future Learning Challenges

Tierney often speaks of "fostering the humility to learn" as a key corporate success factor. And he believes that this humility to learn is at the heart of innovation. Taking on new initiatives in light of—and often in spite of—risk is evidence of Tierney's willingness to question traditional approaches to consulting. Considering the accelerating obsolescence of learning, he suggests that professional service firms like Bain & Company make questioning the status quo the way they do business. Tierney, however, tempers his appetite for change with a cautionary note: "By all means, drive the organization to create. But our business pushes us to be more adaptive than inventive. There is little institutional value to the first mover. Consequently, we build our business around sifting, synthesizing, and adapting. We are adaptive learning leaders."

Tierney speculates that as far as the future is concerned, managing organizational complexity as a function of Bain's growth and diversification will be an important training issue for senior management to tackle.

As a consulting firm, Bain relies heavily on a "train the trainer" model, employing its own consultants as training leaders. Bain's practice of relying heavily on Bain consultants and senior management as trainers and program directors has been criticized by both insiders and external training experts as inefficient and expensive.

Tierney is adamant in committing Bain's case-team and firm leadership resources to flagship programs. "The consultant trainer pool will grow in proportion to the numbers we have to train," he says. "But that's a complexity issue, not a scale issue. It is and will continue to be expensive. But consider the value! Our internal data show us that our partners rank being a trainer as one of the most outstanding activities of their careers. I would never want to go to a cadre of professional trainers to do the bulk of our training. I want consultants, managers, senior partners *all* involved in training. As trainers they learn more. They become more integrated and committed to the firm's goals and values. They come back from the programs truly energized. They show their student colleagues what it means to be a committed teacher-learner! This has been my experience at Bain. This is who we are and how we succeed."

Michael Dell Takes Leadership Personally

At Dell Computer, championing learning is more fundamental than sponsorship. It's about the direction you set and the things you measure. Each year, CEO Michael Dell hosts an all-employee (and family) event in the company's hometown of Austin, Texas. That has required hiring an arena that seats tens of thousands. For the past three years, one message from Michael Dell has been consistent—that the key to the future is in its people.

This message has been a constant theme of the CEO, and every top leader in the company has picked up the mantra. It's no surprise that items like Management and Leadership Development appear on the list of critical business issues for most Dell managers.

If Michael Dell makes clear that learning is expected, he also demonstrates that it is *inspected*. For example, when the company mandated that all managers take instruction on ethics, values, and the legal aspects of management, Dell sent personal e-mails to his team, letting them know that he expected 100 percent of managers to meet the requirement. He requested updates on a regular basis, detailing who was on track for compliance with the mandate. The heads of those organizations that were falling behind got e-mails from the CEO. Some got phone calls. The few individuals not yet in compliance with the annual requirement got personal notes as the year neared its end. The target got hit.

Dell vice chairmen Kevin Rollins and Mort Topfer are also champions of learning. For years the training function has had its own operations review with them. At these quarterly meetings the Vice Chairman has been known to express concern that the company may not be investing enough or doing enough in the area of training, a marked contrast to top officers at most companies whose main concerns would be cost, improvements in productivity, and reductions in the average cost of learning.

Jim Vanderslice, the newest member of the Office of the Chairman (having joined in December of 1999) says: "As an individual, I have always felt that education is an ongoing process; it is a verb, not a noun. The same is true for an organization. The individuals within an organization have to view learning and skill development as an integral part of their development and contribution to the organization. Although it is the individual's responsibility, education should be facilitated by the organization and encouraged at the most senior level."

This "marketing" role for training extends to other members of the top executive team. Ro Parra, senior vice president of Dell's Public and Americas International Group, is a good example. Says Parra: "Every executive has a role when it comes to training and education. It's to lead by example. You have to make learning a priority. One of the best ways to do that is to make sure that, when there are budget pressures, training is the last thing to be cut." Parra does lead by example. He's known for being slow to cut back on training, even in the tightest of times.

A good measure of his leadership by example may be in Parra's approach to a key sales training initiative he sponsored in his business. After a series of specific memos to his team leading up to the training program, he met with his management team on the eve of the event.

In that meeting, Parra first outlined what he intended to do during and after the training program to encourage learning and to coach improved performance. He then worked with his management team until each of them had a similar plan. Perhaps most important, they saw him start implementing his plan when he personally kicked off the training the next day.

Parra markets training in another important way too. He insists on getting reports on the success of training programs in his business, and he reports on those successes to his peers on the company's executive committee. More than once this practice has led other execs to implement similar training interventions.

However, chronicling the efforts of the Office of the Chairman at Dell Computer Corporation must not be allowed to give the impression that these officers are the dominant and solitary forces in the marketing of training in the company. Much of that work is done by the leaders of the various Dell businesses and functions.

As Rollins observes, "We clearly must have a robust training roadmap and resources to deliver, but the priorities are never clear when you look at the total company. There are many different areas with different priorities appropriate for each. The needs are down in the business and must be developed by those much closer to the action. I think as the Office of the Chairman we can set training as a priority and an important element of keeping the company on track, but the trade-offs as to how much training and what kinds must be made by people closer to the front line. It is like our mandate to hire the best. We certainly want it and preach it, but the hiring doesn't get done at our level. Training is the same to me."

Rollins also rejects setting global targets for training, saying, "We have tried to set a number of hours of training, but that worked poorly. What do you include? Sales meetings? New product training? Orientation?" The vice chairman concludes, "I think the best companies break training needs down to very finite levels within organizations and put the responsibility for making it happen, as with the entire P&L, at the General Manager level." But he does add, "Tons of prodding and positive reinforcement from the top will help."

While the business benefits to the company are clear, what may be more important is something much subtler. Learning is a part of how Dell Computer Corporation does business. The visible example of the CEO is not considered any more remarkable than his involvement in the financial management of the company or its technology roadmap.

At a recent executive conference, Topfer outlined five major challenges for the future. Chief among them was developing people. Said Topfer, "Our hiring requirements also demand ongoing training and development in a fast-changing environment, including a better understanding of why we do business the way we do. Sixty percent of our more than twenty-three thousand corporate and Americas employees are new to the company within the past two years. Go back a third year, and the number increases to nearly 80 percent. In fact, 30 percent of the Americas vice presidents attending this meeting didn't even work at Dell when the last global VP conference was held.

"My message is that, even in an entrepreneurial culture, our people are best able to do their jobs and help the company to the next plateau when they have a fundamental understanding of where we've come from, how and why. The transfer of that knowledge has to begin with all of us."

Active Support in Marketing at STMicroelectronics University

Pasquale Pistorio of STMicroelectronics been an personal advocate for learning through much of his career. ST now has more than 350 experts, teachers, and certified trainers who spread the word as "ambassadors" of learning. However, Pistorio, who earlier in his career rose through Motorola's ranks from salesman to director of world marketing, is the individual who serves as the chief marketing agent for ST's learning culture.

Pistorio and his top executives offer active support by trumpeting and reinforcing the strategic role of ST University at press conferences. "As a missionary," says Pistorio, "I have been the most vocal supporter of the initiative." He preaches internally on the importance of knowledge sharing and education, pushing the organization to learn continuously and to spread ideas and best practices.

During interviews or speeches Pistorio systematically mentions the importance of ST's people. For instance, the most memorable line for employees from a recent Pistorio speech describing his vision of the company's organizational trends is, "The secret of our success is in our major resource: PEOPLE, PEOPLE, PEOPLE."

Most of the time, the CEO attends important events such as certification or recognition ceremonies for team members, good suggestion makers, and speakers organized by ST University. When ST University's new campus in Fuveau, France was completed, Pistorio was one of the first executives to visit the center. He has delivered speeches on both occasions when ST University inaugurated new buildings. In addition to speechmaking at these ceremonies, he stresses the importance of ST University and employee education during his interviews with the media.

Many of ST's competitors have their own corporate universities, the units charged with developing company culture and helping bind together organizations which are more cellular, multicultural, and global. As their own corporate university got off the ground in 1994, people from ST University extensively surveyed other existing corporate universities. They visited major competitors like Intel and Motorola and several others in totally different fields such as Accor Group, Volkswagen, and Ford. ST University's people got new ideas they could apply in a semiconductor industry environment and established benchmarks for the highest standards for corporate universities.

Marketing ST University inside the Company

From the onset, ST University was conceived as a product complete with branded image, five-year plan, and communication plan describing its objectives and benefits. Innovation is important not only in the microelectronics business, but also in the ways of educating people and considering learning. ST University markets itself inside the company through eight different channels:

- Paper catalog: courses, schedule, location
- Home page: in ST intranet system and through ST Internet site
- E-mail: normal communication, promotion
- Newsletter: including ST's corporate newsletter and ST University's newsletter
- STMicroelectronics web site
- Conferences produced by the university

- Trade shows attended: 5 in 1999 (worldwide)
- Advertising: articles publications (specific and national).

ST University has enjoyed success for several reasons. It projects a strong and consistent brand so all employees can immediately recognize ST University. The marketing plan addresses and caters to distinct market segments such as employees, managers, and external organizations. Its clear mission states that the strategic role of ST University is to focus on corporate issues and to support and advise the local training departments in establishing guidelines. The ST University central training center is close to ST's leading-edge-technology wafer factory at Rousset, near Aix-en-Provence in southern France. Students have the opportunity to study at an impressive, well-equipped campus especially designed for learning. This environment helps foster an ST company culture among like-minded, forward-looking participants.

Having internal company speakers share their expertise with peers is vital. It gives more credibility to the training courses and complements theory taught by either ST University staff or academic partners with practical company experience. Trained employees get the opportunity to immediately see how a concept is put into practice at ST. To establish the foundation for a dynamic and effective corps of in-house trainers, ST University created a trainer certification process.

Being close to the reality of everyday life in the company, ST University-certified trainers and speakers offer a comprehensive network of shared competencies and common experience across all the company's locations. CEO Pistorio views the concept of "ST Trains ST" as a key to the company's success at ST Microelectronics University because "it allows the internal trainers, who are company experts teaching for a portion of their time, to conceptualize their experience and motivate the trainees by showing management commitment."

This group of certified trainers multiplies the effect of ST University's training efforts. In-house trainers accelerate the learning process and create an economy of scale in which hundreds more employees become acculturated to ST, learn common tools and methods, and communicate better. ST University also certifies "internal consultants" who help coach and develop work teams under the Team@ST program.

When ST University was first opened, despite the officially announced support of the top management, many employees needed convincing that it was not just a fad, but a real attempt to support training and education. When the first programs succeeded, managers embraced the "ST Trains ST" principle, and the company achieved greater efficiency. This convinced more of ST's business units, which then appealed to ST University for help in developing learning programs to support their strategies.

On some occasions, the CEO has directly involved himself in employee education by asking ST University to develop a specific course to forcefully and rapidly address an important issue. The CEO frequently encourages his staff to personally involve themselves in employee education by teaching. The top management's presence greatly enriches ST University's faculty and offers tremendous support to the learning function. ST University's strong focus on management development has greatly enhanced the ability of managers to perform their roles. When the CEO proposes increasing the ST University budget with direct financial support from the various business units, ST University gets the resources it needs to develop courses and recruit the best trainers. By often mentioning the importance of education in his speeches, Pistorio affirms the company's learning culture and helps spread it across the organization.

Due to Pistorio's championing the cause, everyone at ST now clearly sees that training is a strategic initiative. Having the CEO play this multifaceted role has been crucial to the company's commitment to transform itself into a learning organization.

New Business Challenges,
New Learning Initiatives at "R" Us University

Chief executives also become chief advocates for learning when changing business conditions and increased competition dictate a course correction. CEOs heading a company in transition take a personal interest in training (or retraining, as is often the case) employees to upgrade basic skills and realign training activities with the updated business model.

Such is the case at Toys "R" Us, a retailer that has seen its share of market turbulence in recent years. The company's new CEO, John Eyler, has a much greater interest in learning than did his predecessor. Eyler has undertaken a redesign of Toys "R" Us stores, added private label products to its inventory for the first time, and struck a partnership with Scholastic magazine. Seeking access to the educational toy market, Toys "R" Us bought Imaginarium, a maker of educational toys. "We've reinvented ourselves—make that reinvigorated," says Fay O'Dell, manager of corporate education.

According to O'Dell, Toys "R" Us management is supportive of educational programs at the company's corporate university, "R" US University. Eyler's vision is to link business goals to education and use education to help drive sales for the company. As O'Dell says, "When you've been a successful company, and it incurs change, it can take a while to understand what has changed. Eyler looks at ways we need to change to stay competitive." Among the training programs under development are sales and service training to integrate its remodeled stores,

Toys "R" Us also upgraded its education support, upgrading the company's tuition reimbursement plan to cover courses at any accredited college or university up to $5,000 a year in tuition expense—double the previous reimbursement for education expenses. Long-term plans call for creating a certificate course in retailing, covering business courses retail management skills. The near-term goals are also specific, according to O'Dell. "We want better product knowledge added as a training strategy, and we want to get our guests (customers) involved and our vendors actively involved" in the new look of retailing at Toys "R" Us. Eventually, Toys "R" Us will have stores with six or seven different formats or marketing themes.

For all of these goals to be achieved, "There must be communication from the top," O'Dell maintains. CEO Eyler has been a visible advocate, leading a series of management strategy meetings involving the entire corporate office at Toys "R" Us.

Avon: Using Marketing to Drive Learning

Another retailer with a long history, Avon Products Inc., also has ambitious plans for its future growth, led by new CEO Andrea Jung. Among other initiatives, Jung has organized a number of leadership development workshops to communicate business goals to Avon's field staff. Claire Neely, Avon's e-learning technologist, says the objective of these seminars is to integrate training with the company's vision of itself tomorrow. As Neely says, "Learning and education goals are not distinct from corporate goals. We are now saying: if that is what your goal is, what do we need to do in education or training to reach those goals? One goal is what Avon calls the "perfect order," an order filled and shipped with no errors or problems. The right items, packed and shipped on schedule."

Avon is evolving from a company with a high relationship culture and one sales channel to a company with multiple sales channels. As Neely explains: "Our goal in 2001 is to take that relationship culture and reinvigorate it, by building a network or structure to support knowledge sharing." One problem Avon will have to deal with over the next five to 10 years is the prospect of losing much of its shared knowledge as many of its long time sales representatives approach retirement age. For Avon, the problem is trying to retain the company's history and culture (the "how we do it" at Avon), while adapting to a new, more competitive market.

Avon is moving toward a new business model with multiple sales channels, new product lines, and new training/education requirements. Direct sales through Avon representatives will still be a factor, though a smaller percentage of total sales volume and sales revenue. "We're creating a different brand for retail distribution, with a different logo and new brand image," Neely explains. "The aim is to create a store within a store, and link that storefront to the community, by stressing health issues such as breast cancer awareness and educating consumers through guest speakers." As with Toys "R" Us, new marketing channels and new product lines will have to be supported through continued training. It's a job ready made for CEO involvement in a visible role as marketing agent and catalyst for learning.

Chapter Summary

Chief executives perform an important function by serving as public ambassadors for learning, or the chief marketing agent for learning in their organizations. Visible CEO support lends credibility to learning programs, and provides encouragement to other senior executives. Through their public announcements, internal memos and e-mails, and annual reports to shareholders, CEOs make a powerful statement about the importance they attach to learning activities within the organization.

Action Steps: CEO as Marketing Agent— Communicate, communicate, communicate

1. Keep your senior executives up to date about learning activities. If you have an internal public relations group, utilize their expertise to keep top executives informed about on-going projects.

2. Educate senior executives through a Corporate University Annual Report of current year projects and next year's planned activities. Send a copy to each senior executive with a summary cover letter.

3. Build a strategic marketing and communications plan for the corporate university.

4. Urge internal marketing stakeholders to develop a single brand to communicate the benefits of continuous learning

5. Remember executive support can be taken away as easily as it is given.

Communicating the Value of a Corporate University

Strategic learning and organization-wide performance enhancement are keys to sustaining an organization's competitive advantage. Communicating this value to senior management is central to a corporate university's mission. Senior managers will support learning activities with widespread employee participation. But if you cannot stimulate employee participation, the arduous tasks of achieving senior management buy-in—and creating a strategic learning infrastructure—are wasted efforts. What if you gave a class and no one came?

One target of internal marketing is the customers—the employees who stand to benefit directly from learning offerings. Another focus of marketing efforts is the senior executives and business unit leaders. You must demonstrate that learning is an integral and indispensable part of the business. You can settle for a tactical, "throw it out there and see what sticks" kind of marketing, or you can develop a strategic marketing plan. Strategic marketing allows you to tie together different services so that you are consistently building on successes as you prepare for the future.

Your strategic marketing plan should include marketing objectives that answer the following questions:

Who is the target audience?

What are the objectives (desired outcomes) of the marketing plan?

Where will we implement our marketing (posters, e-mail, presentations, etc.)

When do we need to begin the marketing plan?

How long should the marketing plan last and HOW much should we spend?

The plan should be easy to follow, beginning at a very high level and then identifying detailed communication and marketing activities. For example, Booz Allen corporate university, The Center for Performance Excellence, has the following objectives as its strategic marketing goal: increasing awareness, influencing behavior and building the image of a world-class corporate university providing a suite of learning opportunities for Booz Allen employees.

Some of Booz Allen's marketing objectives include:

Focus	Objective
The Center Itself	Continue to expand brand recognition internally and externally
Individuals and their Managers	Communicate the link between competencies and learning options for staff and managers so staff members will be able to participate in the programs and services that meet their personal development plan needs
All Employees	Promote use of the Booz Allen Virtual Campus so employees have up-to-date information regarding programs and services
Technical Staff	Promote the new technology training center programs to increase awareness of online and instructor-led options
Senior Executives	Communicate the Executive Excellence Center's strategic plan to gain support for design and development of new programs and services
	Gain external recognition so the credibility of the Center for Performance Excellence increases.

Source: Booz-Allen & Hamilton

Endnotes
Is Your CEO Ready For The Knowledge Economy?

The CEOs profiled in this book share a common belief: they see continuous learning as a first order of strategy making. In fact, many CEOs are saying there are no longer any training issues, there are only business strategy issues. That principle, along with a strong belief in the business-critical role of learning, fosters the climate within their companies.

Traditionally, training managers have focused on aligning training to business goals. While this is crucial, alignment must be considered a two-way issue. It is not enough for a training manager to simply devise strategies for alignment with business goals and then pronounce the job done. Concurrently, the CEO must be engaged in thinking how learning and human capital can achieve growth for the business. For example, when James Wolfensolf, President of the World Bank announced, "We need to become in effect a "Knowledge Bank," a series of transformations happened: an investment in groupware, the appointment of a Chief Information Officer, the launch of a knowledge management program and the strategic management of learning under the direction of a Chief Learning Officer. [1]

CEOs who think like Wolfensolf are convinced that investing in learning *can* and *will* change their business. Hence they devote personal time to understanding how their business and their industry will evolve as the Knowledge Economy unfolds. And by both exhortation and example, they encourage their managers do the same.

Seven Lessons Needed For
The CEO In The Knowledge Economy

CEOs who operate as The Chief Education Officer for their organization live out seven lessons of involvement:

Lesson #1: Create and promote a vision for learning

Lesson #2: Identify and communicate how an education investment achieves business goals

Lesson #3: Develop an Advisory Board to support, direct and review your company's education function

Lesson #4: Identify Subject Matter Experts and build real-time links from business issues to training

Lesson #5: Promote the importance of using your CEO as faculty to celebrate and spread the culture of the organization

Lesson #6: Profile CEOs in your company's industries that operate as "Learning CEOs." Top management learns best from their peers

Lesson #7: Encourage your CEO to be the Chief Spokesperson for Learning.

In addition to these seven lessons of involvement, CEOs need to exhibit a certain level of enthusiasm and engagement for how learning assists the organization in meeting its business goals. In their day-to-day roles, CEOs must also exhibit five key behaviors if they are going to lead their organization in the Knowledge Economy. These behaviors include:

1) Create clarity of purpose for why learning is key to achieve business goals

2) Become the Chief Marketing Agent promoting the value of learning

3) Spend quality time on how an investment in education will achieve business goals

4) Work closely with the Chief Learning Officer of the organization

5) Push the organization to develop a world-class learning function.

Now let's look at each of these behaviors in detail to see what CEOs must do to prepare their organization for the Knowledge Economy.

Create Clarity Of Purpose For Learning

CEOs need to do more than be committed to learning: they must be totally involved in directing their organization to use learning to achieve business goals. One way to get this done is for CEOs to "develop goals" for the business. For example, when Dell Learning created the Dell Board of

Regents, Michael Dell set a goal that each employee have a training and personal development plan in place each year. This plan was to be reviewed by the employee's manager and clear training initiatives were to be identified in the plan. One example of a training initiative that soon became the company mantra was the launch of a new programs known as, "Know The Net," an online self-paced training program which is an overview of the Dell Business Model. Completion of the program earns each Dell employee a certificate entitled Michael Dell Says I Know The Net. This type of acknowledgement of continuous learning sends a clear message to employees: learning is tied to success on-the-job performance.

Become the Chief Marketing
Agent promoting the value of learning

In speeches, reports, meetings and public appearances, CEOs signal their beliefs about the importance of continuous learning to the organization. Perhaps the most vocal spokesperson for learning is Jack Welch, CEO of General Electric. Welch reinforces his commitment to training by constantly promoting the sharing of best practices through workouts or knowledge sharing at Crotonville, General Electric Management Development Institute. Whenever Welch hears from a divisional President about a successful project, he asks, "What have you done to share your success and learning with other divisions?" In this way he not only signals his interest in learning but he also sets expectations of collective learning and transfer of best practices within he organization. [2]

Spend quality on how an investment
in education will achieve business goals.

CEOs are busy people with many demands on their time, but "Learning CEOs" involve themselves in the education and development area. They spend quality time engaged in thinking and sometimes even writing about how an investment in education will impact their company and their entire industry. This has certainly been the case for Jack Welch who, as this book is going to the printer, is finishing up on a book about his leadership at General Electric, focusing on his time as a teacher and learner at Crotonville. Committing time also means becoming involved in a company's Training Board of Advisors, as Michael Dell has done to ensure he is reviewing, supporting and directing the company's investment in learning. Above all, spending time means setting a clear example for colleagues regarding the importance of education within the company.

Work closely with the Chief Learning Officer

The latest research from Corporate University Xchange, *Chief Learning Officers: Running Education as a Business*, shows that of 175 CLOs interviewed, almost twenty percent report directly to the CEO. A good relationship between the CEO and Chief Learning Officer, either formal or informal, is key to ensuring that a company's investment in education is exploited as a competitive advantage. In fact, John Coné, the President of Dell Learning relates his surprise at finding that Michael Dell put himself on the interview team when it came time to hire the head of Dell Learning. Says Coné, "I have to admit that the first time I met Michael, I was impressed with how engaged he was on the subject of learning. *He* spent as much time asking me what he could do as he did asking what I expected to bring to the function of President of Dell Learning. A big part of my decision to join Dell was knowing that I had an ally in the CEO who was willing to be hands-on in the education area."

Push the organization to
develop a world-class learning function

Finally, the CEO must be a believer in learning and support and fund the development of a world-class education function. This means that the CEO sponsors the development of a business case, which outlines the vision, scope and strategy behind launching a world-class education function. In other words, the CEO creates the same set of standards for the education function that he has for any new business initiatives at the company. This business-focus gives credibility to a company's investment in education.

Why are CEOs pushing for more training? "Not to be altruistic," states Corey Jack, Head of Bank of Montreal Institute For Learning. Instead they want to meet business strategies and use the investment as a competitive advantage in attracting and retaining the best employees.

How Can Your CEO Become A Learning CEO?

Are you ready to encourage your CEO to become A Learning CEO? The seven lessons in this book outline the path, but it's your journey, so first talk and rub shoulders with other training managers who have worked with and been supported by active CEOs. The Appendix of the book outlines with whom you can benchmark with in order to learn not only what was done but also how to avoid the roadblocks and barriers you may encounter along the way. Good Luck, and keep me posted. I can be reached at jcm@corpu.com.

—Jeanne C. Meister

APPENDIX

ABOUT CORPORATE
UNIVERSITY XCHANGE

Founded in 1995 by Jeanne C. Meister, Corporate University Xchange, Inc. is a New York City-based corporate education and research firm, offering products and services to help training professionals optimize their organization's learning function. With a client base from around the world representing a broad spectrum of industries, as well as institutions of higher education, Corporate University Xchange is considered the specialist for corporate university development and management.

The leader in providing e-learning market intelligence and continuing education for corporate educators, Corporate University Xchange helps learning and development professionals create and implement breakthrough human capital strategies.

Is Your CEO a Chief Education Officer?

The purpose of this questionnaire is to assess the level of involvement the CEO has in the everyday operation of your company's corporate university.

1. In what ways is your CEO an education visionary?
2. How many educational programs, if any, has your CEO sponsored?
3. Does your CEO regularly teach or facilitate training sessions?
4. How does your CEO market and promote corporate education?
5. In what areas do you consider your CEO to be an expert?
6. Does your CEO occupy a seat on the corporate training board?
7. Is your CEO an active listener, observer, and overall learner?
8. To which function/individual does the corporate learning function report?
9. How many levels separate the corporate learning function from the CEO in your organization?
10. How has CEO involvement in corporate learning promoted:
    a. The learning function?
    b. The company as a whole?
    c. The company's leadership position in the industry?

Featured Companies

Avon Products Incorporated
1345 Avenue of the Americas
New York, NY 10105-0196
CEO: Andrea Jung
www.avon.com

Bain & Company
2 Copley Place
Boston, MA 02116
CEO: Len Banos
www.bain.com

Booz-Allen & Hamilton
8283 Greensboro Dr.
McLean, VA 22102
CEO: Ralph W. Shrader
www.bah.com

Buckman Laboratories
1256 N. Mclean Blvd.
Memphis, TN 38108-0305
CEO: Steven B. Buckman
www.buckman.com

Conoco Incorporated
600 N. Dairy Ashford
Houston, TX 77079
CEO: Archie W. Dunham
www.conoco.com

Dell Computer Corporation
1 Dell Way
Round Rock, TX 78682-2222
CEO: Michael Dell
www.dell.com

Deutsche Bank
Taunusanlage 12
60262 Frankfurt, Germany
CEO: Rolf E. Breuer
www.deutsche-bank.de

General Electric
3135 Easton Tpke.
Fairfield, CT 06431-0001
CEO: Jack Welch
www.ge.com

First Union Corporation
One First Union Center
Charlotte, N.C. 28288-0013
CEO: G. Kennedy Thompson
www.firstunion.com

Deutsche Lufthansa
Von-Gablenz-Strasse 2-6
D-50679 Cologne 21, Germany
CEO: Jürgen Weber
www.lufthansa.com

NCR Corporation
1700 S. Patterson Blvd.
Dayton, OH 45479

CEO: Lars Nyberg
www.ncr.com

Memorial Hermann Healthcare System
9401 Southwest Freeway
Houston, TX 77074
CEO: Dan S. Wilford
www.mhhs.org

STMicroelectronics
20 Route de Pre-Bois, ICC Bldg.
CH-1215 Geneva 15, Switzerland
CEO: Pasquale Pistorio
www.st.com

Tennessee Valley Authority
400 W. Summit Hill Dr.
Knoxville, TN 37902
CEO: Craven Crowell
www.tva.gov

Toys "R" Us
461 From Road
Paramus, NJ 07652
CEO: John H. Eyler
www.toysrus.com

United Technologies Corporation
One Financial Plaza
Hartford, CT 06103
CEO: George David
www.utc.com

FOOTNOTES

Chapter Two

1) "Anticipating Welch on Welch," **New York Times** November 29, 2000 page B-1.

2) "The Ways Chief Executive Officers Lead," Harvard Business Review, May-June 1996 pages 59-72.

3) Interview between Steven Tallman former Vice President of Training, Bain & Company and Thomas Tierney, Managing Director.

4) Interview between Sheldon Ellis, Vice President, Bulab Learning Center, and Bob Buckman CEO, Buckman Laboratories.

5) Interview between John Coné, VP Dell. President Dell Learning and Michael Dell, CEO, Dell Computer Corporation.

6) Robert Slater, **Jack Welch's Battle Plan for Corporate Revolution, The GE Way Fieldbook,** (McGraw-Hill) page 89.

7) Dan S. Wilford. **Trust Matters: New Directions in Healthcare Leadership**" page 25.

Chapter Three

1) "The Job No CEO should Delegate." Larry Bossidy, Harvard Business Review March 2001, page 49.

In an interview with Harvard Business Review, Larry Bossidy, former Chairman and CEO of Allied Signa, reported devoting between thirty to forty percent of each day for the first two years on the job to hiring and developing leaders at the company. While that is a huge job for a CEO to devote to any single task, the results at Allied Signal speak for themselves. In the eight years of Bossidy's tenure as CEO (1991-1999), return on equity increased from 10% to 28%, but perhaps the best measure of the quality of Allied Signal executives was the fact that several were recruited to lead other organizations. Dan Burnham became CEO of Raytheon and Fred Poses CEO of American Standard. Both launched a corporate learning center similar to the one at Allied Signal where they had received their continuing management education.

2.) Jeffrey Garten, **The Mind of the CEO**, (Basic Books) page 111.

Endnotes

1) Michael Earl and David Fenny, "How To Be a CEO for the Information Age," Sloan Management Review, Winter 2000, page 15.

2) Ibid, page 17.